AF270548

EFFECTIVE

MELISSA SWIFT

EFFECTIVE

HOW TO DO GREAT WORK IN A FAST-CHANGING WORLD

WILEY

Library of Congress Cataloging-in-Publication Data is Available:

ISBN 9781394377497 (Cloth)
ISBN 9781394377503 (ePub)
ISBN 9781394377510 (ePDF)

Cover Design: Wiley
Cover Image: © RLT_Images/Getty Images
Author Photo: Courtesy of the Author

SKY10151560_040226

*To Artem and Mira, whose love is
the best thing in my life.*

Contents

Contents

I wrote this book to answer the number one question people asked me after my first book, *Work Here Now*.

All too often, I'd give a talk on some of its themes around broken work, or I'd meet someone in real life who'd read it, and they'd say something like:

> *Okay, Melissa, I get it and I agree: the world of work is kind of a mess these days, and based on what you wrote I understand how and why that's happening.*
> *But tell me: knowing all of that, what should I do differently?*

It's a poignant question. Work goes through historical cycles of being more and less difficult, and hoo boy, is the old work roller coaster in a dip right now. Not since the early Industrial Revolution, I'd argue, have we seen such crummy working conditions. The specifics have changed—swap out dingy, flammable factories for endless Zoom calls and chat pings—but in the AI age we're really in a pickle, much as we were when we first started industrialized production. It's rough out there.

And what's worse is that workforce/workplace issues are, almost by definition, multi-owner problems. If your day is tricky, it's often the fault of your direct boss, whoever invented the pop-up notification, and dozens of people in between. No one holds the strings of the whole muddle.

So people are, naturally, interested in what they can control. I get that, and I agree!

As a long-time people consultant, I wanted, passionately, to be helpful to this question of what individuals can do. But I was also sensitive to some key divides in the whole discussion of work that keep us from progressing sensibly on the topic.

First, there's endless back and forth about a crudely framed conflict between the interests of the employee (framed as trying to stay mentally and physically healthy) and the interests of the employer (framed as making money for shareholders). Any statement you make about one side is immediately interpreted as a shot fired at the other side. You don't want to prevent people keeling over from burnout? You're messing with my precious return on investment! You want to stay profitable in the long term? You're messing with my employee pickleball courts! Everything is positioned in zero-sum-game terms . . . which has never solved any problem, ever.

Second, within people consulting, there are two very strongly guarded siloes. One is the organizational silo, which concerns itself largely with structural activities, like organization or job design, as well as organization-wide issues like culture or employee experience; the other is the individual development silo, which concerns itself largely with person-by-person activities like coaching and leadership development. Many folks in the field adhere strongly to one side or the other and, similar to the above issue, the bickering gets silly. The organization-side folks get very huffy that nothing will ever get solved unless we fix the broken organizational systems (they're right) and the development-side folks state with great frustration that nothing is ever going to work properly as long as leaders behave like jerks (they're also right). On both sides, there's a lot of "I've studied this micro-topic in detail and discovered that it fixes everything, stop working on whatever topic you thought was important and just focus on my one thing." Also unhelpful.

x

Preface

I was conscious of these divides as I sat down to answer that question of how to work better, as an individual, in a messy world of work. I sought—in the awesome term that Chief Human Resources Officer and professor Courtney Chisholm, interviewed later in this book, just taught me—a "third way." What if we didn't have to see employers and employees as fighting over a limited array of resources? What if we didn't have to work on either whole-organization issues OR individual development? Are there spaces that contain both sides of both arguments?

Effectiveness is one example of that kind of space. It's not the "one thing" that magically fixes everything, but you can see it as a frame around a powerful and varied mosaic of solutions. Effectiveness is where employer and employee interests come together—you want to be great at accomplishing the goals of your job, and your employer wants that too. It's also a place where we can bring together different organizational and developmental thinking to help move people to action. Think about your job like a job designer, but then solve for what to do like a coach! It's a great "third way."

I've marshalled a few different elements in this book to help think through what the "third way" of effectiveness looks like. First, my own experience innovating and consulting in the organizational and development spaces. I've worked with large organizations on very complex problems like mobilizing their workforce for a digital transformation or shaping a central people strategy, and developed a lot of data-driven ways to examine these problems. I've also been a leader in large organizations myself, so I definitely have those battle scars too—and you'll hear some of my painfully won insight in that regard.

But I knew my own brain was not enough. So, you'll see some interesting historical examples and some wonderful scientific and academic research, too. Finally, I had the honor of speaking to more than 20 folks from the corporate world, academia, public service,

Preface

and consulting—all of them multifaceted, boundary-breaking, silo-crossers. Their brilliance, and their spirit, infuses this book with so much more than I could ever have given it on my own.

With all those elements in mind, we'll start by looking, in Chapter 1, at how to think about your work like a people consultant would (and what new insights that brings). Then we'll examine in Chapter 2 four simple elements that each of us bring together to be effective at work: Knowledge, Methods, People, and Technology. In Chapter 3 we'll do a deep dive on Knowledge and Methods, and in Chapter 4 we'll do a deep dive on People and Technology—including how to know where you're strongest, and what disruption looks like for each element. Chapter 5 takes us on a tour through the effectiveness lessons of high-stakes jobs: firefighting, air traffic control, and emergency medicine.

Then we'll flip the script and examine how to best overcome four forces currently challenging people's effectiveness at work: work intensification (Chapter 6), emotional workplaces (Chapter 7), hyper-transparency (Chapter 8), and chaos (Chapter 9). We'll then finish up in Chapter 10 by looking at how to tell when you *can't* be effective (and what to do about it) and examining the future of effectiveness in Chapter 11.

I'm not promising you a silver bullet. This is not a "one thing" book. But in the mosaic I've put together around effectiveness, virtually everyone will find something that helps them.

So, let's go take a look at how we can all do great work.

Part I

Being Effective

Chapter 1

The Simple Power of Being Effective

Being effective is powerful.

You probably know that in January 2025, fires ravaged the Los Angeles area, killing dozens of people and destroying more than 15,000 structures. Two of the fires—Palisades and Eaton—are in the top three most destructive fires the state has ever experienced.[1]

But did you know that meteorologist Edgar McGregor predicted the fires—and in doing so, enabled scores of folks to get out alive?

As McGregor told *People Magazine*, in late December conditions in Los Angeles were eerily similar to those experienced in Lahaina, Maui, and Paradise, California, ahead of devastating fires in those communities. On daily hikes, he could see canyons full of brush ready to burn; the Santa Ana winds would arrive December 30.

He knew fires were coming, and on a local Facebook group, he gave people simple, lifesaving advice. One piece of guidance sticks with me: he told folks to park their cars in their driveways facing out, because the time it takes to back your car out could make the difference between life and death.[2]

His neighbors in Altadena, California, listened. As McGregor told NPR (National Public Radio), at least one family left town entirely in anticipation of the fires. Many others took his advice on preparation and were able to evacuate quickly when the time came.

This master meteorologist, by the way? He was all of 24 years old.

Gratitude flowed in for McGregor's amazing work. His reaction?

"So people are sending me all these comments and I'm thinking to myself, I just did my job."[3]

I just did my job. That's what this book is about: being effective at work.

Nothing fancy and nothing complicated, but done right, it can be amazing—for you and the people around you. In McGregor's case, he was firing on all cylinders as a weather scientist: studying the local conditions, understanding what was coming, and communicating about it in a compelling way to people for whom it really mattered. We see him as a hero because of the lifesaving impact he had, but in a way his humble statement is right on. He just did his job. But really, really well.

We can all do this. We can all be effective—and truly do great work—even in a world where that simple thing has gotten incredibly tough.

This book is about how.

Why Effectiveness, Anyway?

Now, let's get to the question you may be asking right now: who is this lady to tell me how to be effective? She doesn't know my work! And that's a fair comment: humans do an incredibly diverse array of jobs. There are people out there studying cacti and people out there teaching AI to not sound like a weirdo. Work ranges from incredibly manual to incredibly cerebral. Some work is awful, and some work is delightful. (The second part of that statement is a specific reference to a video I recently saw of zookeepers walking a wombat on a leash. *That* is a delightful job.)[4]

But what's interesting is that the nature of being effective, across so many jobs, is fairly consistent. In this book we'll focus on the common threads that can help us all do better, whether you're wrangling wombats or sadly in some other line of work. As a long-time consultant helping organizations get work right—for their own profitability and their employees' sake—I've seen firsthand, over and over, how the same themes play out across geographies and industries. I've also had the privilege of learning about how various academics and professionals take apart this question of being good at your job, and you'll hear from some of those brilliant people in this book too.

I believe that if people knew more about how work was analyzed and studied, they'd actually do their jobs better. So please consider this book a bridge between the working world and the people who study it. Instead of looking from the individual out like most self-development books do, we're going to look from work and jobs inward. Knowing all the ways work is challenging today—and addressing them programmatically—is more than half the battle.

Back to the who-is-this-lady question though: you might also ask, Melissa, *are you, personally, effective?*

Folks, it varies.

I've had what they call a jungle-gym career. I've sold crude oil and I've organized children's parties. I've consulted to the C-suite of giant companies and I've worked a switchboard. I've served as a middle manager for large teams and I've started my own company as the sole employee. I turned down an internship doing the work that has become my passion—people consulting—because I wanted to work in London instead; I returned to the field more than a decade later. I've been woefully underemployed, and I've been sadly over-taxed. I've been terrific and I've been . . . less than terrific.

This is starting to sound like a Traveling Wilburys song. I'll stop.

But I will say this: doing a lot of different work at different kinds of places under very different states of the world, but being the same Melissa, has given me a lot of perspective on what it means to be

The Simple Power of Being Effective

good at what you're doing. Combine that with my professional practice, leading sizeable organizational consulting projects and teams, and I believe I have a unique vantage point into the simple question of what it means to do great work every day.

In case I'm scaring you with all the talk of "great work," this is not a book on always being "Jordan flu game" great. (It might have been a bad pizza, anyway, though that remains controversial.[5]) Extraordinary performance is a wonderful, laudable goal, but *the road to greatness is always going to lead right through being baseline effective*. And for many of us whose achievement drives cause us to constantly skirt burnout, shooting for doing the job as it should be done is a healthier, more productive approach than always trying to knock the cover off the ball.

Let me give you a historical example of how day-to-day effectiveness creates moments of outsize performance. As a frequent speaker, I'm slightly obsessed with how to give better talks. When I learned about the history of one of the greatest speeches of all time, Martin Luther King's "I Have a Dream," it shifted my perspective on how to be good at public speaking. I'd always thought you need some beautiful master script, original and flawless, flowing purely out of your brain alone.

It turns out, the part of the speech we all love was

- improvised on the spot

- somewhat recycled

- prompted by someone in the audience

Listening to King speak to the assembled crowd of a quarter million people, singer Mahalia Jackson exclaimed "Tell 'em about the dream!" She was referring to a speech King had given in Detroit weeks before, in which he painted a compelling picture of a society free of prejudice. At that point, King put his notes away and re-narrated his earlier speech—in a brilliantly fluid and compelling way that completely outdistanced the power of the prior version.[6]

It was a moment of extraordinary greatness built on a foundation of fundamental *effectiveness*. King wrote and spoke constantly; he was always testing new material. He listened to people like Jackson about what was resonating (side note, we all need a Mahalia Jackson in our lives, identifying our best stuff!). He ended up being amazing on that day when it truly mattered, because he was day to day doing the job well.

This is what we're going for!

For me personally, the case for getting the basics of being truly effective hit home a few years ago. With one of the best teams I've ever worked with, I was leading a program on digital transformation leadership for a prominent biotech company. We had lively exercises, terrific speakers, and, most importantly, a wonderful group of leaders in the room. Smart, emotionally clued in, thoughtful.

Those leaders kept telling us something interesting though: they were tired. Very tired. Their jobs were taxing—often featuring a mixture of scientific and operational complexity, not to mention the usual challenges of managing people. They worked for a caring, supportive organization, and it was still tough day to day. Their work was just hard.

And they kept getting called out of the room to deal with some brewing situation in Asia.

Did I mention the date of the program?

February 2020.

So now you know where this story is going.

Within weeks, digital transformation was the least of anyone's concerns. Survival was top of mind as we battled COVID. And these heroic biotech leaders were on the front lines of that war.

7

I wished then, and I still wish now, that I could have those precious days with them back. In my alternate reality, we get down to brass tacks about what would help them do their jobs more easily and effectively. We don't worry, yet, about the higher-order challenges of incorporating digital innovation; we talk about how to get through each day with aplomb. We equip them not for an intriguing future that absolutely did show up, but for the unbelievable test right around the corner.

That experience taught me that the most extreme moments—raging fires, pandemics, a turning point in a social movement—highlight a banal truth.

Effectiveness is the key to so many things.

Get that right and move the world.

The Other Why of Effectiveness

There is, of course, another reason why you'd want to be effective at work.

You'll make more money doing it.

If you ever studied the mathematical concept of compounding in school, you'll understand why this can really add up. Fiduciary firm Life Managed illustrates this idea on their website. A 3% merit increase on a $125,000 salary amounts to a $3,750 raise the first year you get it—but get that same merit increase consistently across 30 years, and you end up making more than $300,000 a year. And you've earned $5.9 million total! ($7.6 million, as they note, if 3% eventually grows to 4% . . .).[7]

This is the exponential beauty of salary math: every bump up gets multiplied against every other bump up. Positioning yourself for what may feel like a less-than-consequential increase has lifetime value. You don't have to pull off a crazy score in any given year—you can make a lot of progress by getting some square shots

Effective

in year over year over year. Building lifetime wealth doesn't take exponential performance; be good at what you do and under decent economic conditions (which may not always be present), you'll do great.

There's another interesting benefit to you of effectiveness, though. Beyond having an impact and making money, feeling like you're accomplishing something actually *protects you from burnout.*

To understand this idea, let's work backward. The widely used and well-validated Maslach Burnout Inventory, which measures workplace burnout for an array of populations, has an entire section on feeling competent at work, entitled "Personal Accomplishment." A sample item might be something like, "I feel I have accomplished many worthwhile things in this job."[8]

What's fascinating about feeling futile as a measure of burnout is the chicken-and-egg question it raises. Do people get burned out and then feel like they're accomplishing nothing, or are they getting burned out because they can't get anything done, and that feels awful?

At a certain point, though—does it matter? If feeling you're getting things done well at least shaves some points off your personal burnout scale, do you care if it's cause or effect?

What Is Your Work?

Before we talk about what it means to be good at your job, we have to talk about knowing what your work is.

This is not a trivial or a rhetorical question. No matter what language you speak, words can mean different things (by themselves or in a string with each other), and job titles and descriptions are built from . . . words. Even very precise, task-by-task accounts of work struggle to capture "task messiness"[9]—or the natural variability that comes when different people do what's allegedly the same thing.

The Simple Power of Being Effective

Even the simplest of nuances in explaining a job can go hilariously wrong. Consider a classic Soviet-era joke:

> *Two mothers are proudly discussing their children's successes. "Vanya has gotten his economics doctorate," says one, "and now he's going to work in the field!"*
>
> *"An economist, like Karl Marx?" exclaims the other.*
>
> *"No," explains the first mom, with a withering stare. "Not an economist like Karl Marx. My son is going to be a SENIOR economist."*

Define Your Work in 10 Easy Steps

There's something inherently tricky about trying to describe work in words. So, we're going to steal a technique from the consulting world—"multi-stakeholder analysis"—to try to get as close as we can to the truth of your job. Amusingly, said technique is also a popular meme—because no one in anyone's life seems to understand what they do.

You're going to use this technique in earnest, though. Here are your 10 steps to do so:

1. Write down in bullet points what you think your job is—off the top of your head. Do not spend more than 10 minutes on this or fill more than one sheet of paper. Then put that sheet of paper away.

2. Next, channel your boss. Again, not spending more than 10 minutes or one sheet of paper, write down how your boss would describe your job. Then put that sheet of paper away too.

3. If you think you have any insight into what your boss's boss thinks your job is, write that down on a separate sheet of

paper. Feel free to skip this step if you truly feel you don't have any insight into what that person thinks.

4. Dedicate the next sheet of paper to your peers. What do they think your job is? Because you're talking about multiple people here, *feel free to capture contradictory information*. As you'll see, that's part of the exercise.

5. If you have an easily identifiable customer, the next sheet is for them. What do they think your job is?

6. If you have people who report to you, capture what they think your job is on the next sheet.

7. If there are any other folks whose opinion of your job matters, such as the general public, go ahead and write down what you believe they think your job is on the next sheet.

8. Finally, go ahead and grab any "official" accounts of your job. Do you have a job description in company systems? Are you part of a union that has legally agreed language describing your job? Are there parts of your job that are mandated by regulation? This is part of your data set too.

9. Now, take out all the pieces of paper. Take a few minutes and look at them together, then note down:

    a. Major points of *resonance*—where do all the different versions line up?

    b. Major points of *dissonance*—where do the various folks who care about your job seriously disagree? Critically, where do they disagree with the original description *you* wrote down? And where does your boss or your boss's boss disagree with other stakeholders, including yourself?

    c. Things that are *interesting* to you—when you looked at your job through others' eyes, do you see anything that makes your brain go "hmmm?"

11

The Simple Power of Being Effective

10. Okay—now go back to step 1. Having looked at your work through an array of stakeholders' eyes, how might you write a sensible page on what it actually is? Make sure you include both *things you agree with* and *things you disagree with* that emerged in your analysis. It's very natural to mentally write out of your job description elements of your job that don't energize you, but being good at your job means being good at the whole hairy mess. Believe me when I say, we'll talk about how to eat some of those less tasty bites later. And note where you could not reconcile multiple views of your job—that's critical data too.

You've Defined Your Work: Here's What to Do Next

So, now you've got yourself a reasonable job description plus some information on where things might be muddled or confusing. How do you feel about it? Are you energized? Are you kind of neutral? Are you completely disgusted?

I will never forget a colleague who was frustrated at a manager's travel approval coming in too late to book a plane ticket exclaiming in horror, "How can you not just go through your inbox and click 'approve' on everything? THAT IS LITERALLY YOUR JOB!" This statement simultaneously struck me as true, and chilling: 24/7 responses to randomly arriving automated approvals was a major part of that senior executive's role, and it really stank for them . . . that's not the work anyone dreams of doing. So if you come out of this exercise feeling genuinely bad about your job, feel free to skip right to Chapter 10, which addresses what you should do when your job and workplace are truly broken.

For everyone else, keep this sheet of paper handy. This will be an important touchstone as we work through how to think about being good at your job, and how to accomplish that under the strange and challenging conditions we now think of as a normal day

12

Effective

at work. Feel free to use it, and the other descriptions you developed for this exercise, to guide other conversations.

Talk to Your Manager About What Your Work *Is*

For example, review what you put together with your manager, and see if it actually aligns with what they think. It might be revealing to show them what you wrote as your best guess as to their beliefs . . . and see how close you were to what they actually think. It's not that there's an exact right version of what you're supposed to be doing, but consciously having the conversation about what the job is can completely change how you talk about performance. And stealing another trick from the consulting playbook, the more alignment, the better. Seeing the world in the same terms means everyone works better.

Compare Work with Your Peers

You can compare work summaries with your peers, too. Some of the most productive conversations I've had about how to do my job better came when I compared notes with peers about *what we actually believed the job to be*; often, everyone is doing the job slightly differently in ways that everyone else can learn from. Or you're all absolutely struggling with the same aspects. It's a fruitful conversation either way. You can diffuse a lot of "you're doing it wrong" energy by first agreeing on what the heck you're all doing.

Compare Your Version of Your Work Against the "Standard" Version

Want even more insight about your work? You can take your description as you've just put it together and compare it to the "standard" version of your job as recorded by the US Government in a fascinating database called O*Net.[10] O*Net uses standardized tasks and criteria to compare jobs against each other.

13

The Simple Power of Being Effective

For instance, in the Work Context section, O*Net measures a criterion called "consequence of error": "How serious would the result usually be if the worker made a mistake that was not easily correctable?" In plain English, how bad is it if you screw up? The jobs that rank the highest on this measure are either medical roles (family physician, ophthalmologist, critical care nurse, pharmacist) or deal with dangerous heavy equipment (construction equipment operators, airfield operators, ship loaders). Make a mistake on these jobs, and lives are lost! It's fascinating to then look at the jobs with the *lowest* consequences for a mistake: tutors, math teachers, dishwashers, and bartenders (some folks might quibble with that last one!).

This level of standardization means that you can look at any job, including your own, in clear terms. I took a look at mine—consultant—which in O*Net is referred to as "Management Analyst." I won't list all 11 tasks associated with my job, but some of them include "Gather and organize information on problems or procedures"; "Document findings of study and prepare recommendations for implementation of new systems, procedures, or organizational changes"; and "Prepare manuals and train workers in use of new forms, reports, procedures or equipment, according to organizational policy." Matching up these admittedly generic accounts of tasks someone in your job might do can be a good gut check as to what you're doing currently. If there's a dramatic mismatch, it might just be that your organization has very specific needs . . . or that something's amiss with the way your job is framed.

It's also interesting to compare your experience of your job to things like the work context or skills required in the "official" O*Net version. As per O*Net's research, 100% of consultants surveyed say they use email every day and 89% say they talk on the phone daily as part of their work. This checks out! O*Net also includes "sociology and anthropology" as part of the consulting skill set, a nuanced insight that I quite like. You don't have to use O*Net's descriptors as

Effective

exact measures, but if there are aspects of your work context that vary wildly (let's say, you're a consultant and not emailing at all . . . which might not be a bad thing . . .) or a listed skill you're not getting to tap into, these are good "food for thought" moments.

Uh Oh: When You've Defined Your Work and You Hate It

There's another sort of "food for thought" moment that often happens here: you look down at the description you've written and exclaim, "Wow, that is NOT what I signed up for when I took this role." This is not uncommon and often happens for positive or at least neutral reasons. Let's look at some reasons why that happens and how you can think about addressing them.

You're Crushing It and/or You Lack Boundaries and Things Got Added to Your Plate

The so-called "curse of competence" is no joke: do things well, and organizations will reward you with . . . more things to do. In a perfect world, increasing responsibility is accompanied in a linear fashion by more money and lots of promotions. In the real world, though, opportunities for better compensation or a more senior role appear unpredictably—and are almost bound to lag actual escalation in what's needed from you. Organizational moves (compensation, promotions) happen on cycles and are constrained by time and funding; changes in work happen minute to minute and never stop coming. In other words, your work can change exponentially faster than anything formally connected to your job. In the near term, this may be fine; in the longer run, it can be a formula for tremendous frustration.

And all of this without layering on the fact that people have different levels of personal accountability. If you've ever watched the show *Below Deck*, in which mysteriously attractive crews shepherd giant yachts through gorgeous parts of the world while battling

The Simple Power of Being Effective

everything from obnoxious guests to overflowing toilets, you'll note a repeated phenomenon: crew members who care more about the end result end up working far more hours than their peers. The crew members who care about bathrooms looking good find themselves up all night cleaning bathrooms. Every job has some version of this, and if you're one of the "insecure overachievers" that the corporate world seeks out, your responsibilities may have quietly exploded over time.

So what do you do in this instance?

First, identify everything you're doing that you believe is not part of your role as it was defined for you. Now, break these activities into actionable categories. Which ones represent a stretch above your role? If you are doing things that are the next level up, of course document them for eventual promotion and compensation purposes. More interesting, to be honest, are activities that are a "diagonal stretch"—potentially taking your career in a slightly different direction toward different kinds of roles. These activities may not have been in your original job description, but they are interesting, different . . . and potentially the future of where your job is going.

Finally, identify stuff that should potentially come off your plate: either things that are low-value-add uses of your time or things that are simply someone else's role. Prepare for some tricky conversations! No one likes to get less-than-entertaining work handed back to them. You may want to approach your manager with a holistic picture of your role, showing how you can be more effective if those responsibilities go back to their rightful owners (or increasingly, get automated). Whatever you do, do NOT accept the excuse of "But you're so good at it!" Your job and your capabilities are two different things. Your capabilities matched against the right version of your job both makes the most money for your organization, and makes you the happiest. Be tough in getting to that win–win.

16

Effective

Changes in Business Strategy or Organizational Structure Shifted Your Role

When the change in your role is more about the organization than you, at least in the near term you'll focus more on adapting than advocating for yourself. Some frequent versions of this scenario include taking on more responsibilities due to others on your team being laid off, or relating to a customer differently (more or less directly) because your organization has reorganized how it goes to market. Or there's a reorganization and all the chairs shuffle. (Sometimes repeatedly . . .)

So what do you do in this instance?

You'll want to think this through using two lenses: what's temporary vs. permanent and what's truly consequential vs. can be allowed to slide. Success here depends on focusing your energy on the most lasting and important changes, not things that are likely to quickly fade away or not affect your day-to-day too much. For example, let's say your organization cuts a bunch of middle managers, but you're not included in the layoffs. Relieved to keep your job, you sit down with your manager to find that you now manage a few more people, are newly responsible for a once-a-year audit around some key data, are taking a point position on some initiatives for the next few months, and have been added to a 30-minute weekly staff meeting for another team.

While this sounds like a lot, focusing on what's lasting and important can help you parse out the path forward. The audit is once a year, so it's not hugely important to your day-to-day; the staff meeting is annoying (who wants another meeting?) but not a huge time commitment. While taking point on more initiatives is challenging in the near term, it's not lasting. This leaves the added people management, which is worth focusing on as a true change in your job—consequential and lasting. Engage with your manager and others about the support you need to take on more people. This support

The Simple Power of Being Effective

could take an array of forms, so it's worth being creative in what you ask for. Do you want more training on managing people? An earlier heads up on HR processes because you're now putting more inputs through? A succession planning discussion about how a trusted member of your team might eventually manage some of the added folks? Getting to a crisp level of specificity about the changes that matter—and the help you need to do a changed job well—can get you through what is on face often a tough scenario.

Changes in Technology Shifted Your Role

Not to scare you, but this scenario is happening in virtually everyone's workplace, right now. In spades. There are the exciting changes in what's possible utilizing fast-evolving AI technology, and there are also the sneaky changes that have happened—and continue to happen—due to much less futuristic technology. For example, as I wrote about in *Work Here Now*, the development of electronic medical records quietly rocked doctors' worlds . . . they now spend as much time dealing with record systems as they spend with the average patient. Scarily, doctors spend 15 minutes on each component, which seems like a lot of time with a computer and not a lot of time with a sick human.[11] Self-checkout is another good everyday example. The key tasks of checking someone out at a supermarket or drugstore—everything from scanning items to processing credit cards—have been, in many instances, handed over to the customer. What's left for the checkout worker is a somewhat motley assortment of tasks: ad hoc IT support for customers who struggle with self-checkout functionality, chasing down would-be thieves who refuse to pay for the goods they've scanned, or just hanging out near the registers being a friendly face. It didn't take advanced AI to radically transform that particular job.

So what do you do in this instance?

Ooh, the [digital] ink that has been spilled trying to answer this question. "How can you remain relevant in a world of fast-moving technology? Can you change your skill set fast enough? Is AI going to take your job? IS YOUR JOB GONE AND YOU JUST DON'T KNOW IT YET BECAUSE AI DIDN'T TELL YOU?" If you listen to the cacophony of pundits—and it's hard not to because they are screaming all over LinkedIn and a host of other platforms—they will tell you that you need to aggressively reskill and upskill yourself, like, yesterday. Dig a bit deeper and this recommendation often devolves into lists of fairly flat online courses . . . womp womp. If you're someone who learns well that way, go for it. But 90% of us don't finish the dang courses![12]

Most of us, in fact, learn like crows, who are notoriously clever about building and using tools—even tools that are combinations of other tools. How do crows learn? They play around with things and have fun. They get an actual kick out of deploying technology (sticks in their case): "[Crows] are in a better mood after using a tool to get a reward versus not using a tool to get the same reward."[13] This is hugely analogous to humans in the workplace. Borrowing from Herminia Ibarra's groundbreaking thinking on how identity shifts when we play with new identities—trying them on like kids playing dress-up—your journey into a future where your job may be quite different should lead through some "sandbox" moments with the technology that is coming.

If you're not being provided an opportunity to toy around with new technologies, ask for one . . . or find one outside of work. I once worked with a ball bearings company that needed to expand its robotics capability. They were about to go out and hire high-priced talent from other companies, but someone suggested surveying their own employees. Lo and behold, they had at least a dozen folks who were serious robotics enthusiasts . . . and had

The Simple Power of Being Effective

developed all the right future-forward skills on Saturdays and Sundays in their garages. Those folks became the core of the new robotics team—and believe me when I say, they were pretty jazzed about it.

As Chapter 1 Draws to a Close . . .

At the end of every chapter of this book, you'll see three categories of summary recommendations. First, there are recommendations for everyone that make sense no matter where you are in the organization. Second, there are recommendations if you are the boss—what should you do with the learning in this chapter if you do in fact manage other people. Finally, if you have a meaningful degree of control over an organization or part of one, then the "if you're the big boss" recommendations are for you.

For everyone

- *Do the work to understand what your job is—from a bunch of perspectives.* It's a simple paradigm shift, but thinking about what's in your job for a few minutes, instead of your performance of that job, might yield just the a-ha you've been looking for. If you use the exercise earlier in this chapter, where you consciously record what other folks might think you should be doing all day, then blind spots, trouble spots, and yes—some brilliant spots too—should emerge. The first step to being amazing at your job is understanding exactly what your job is . . . and that is *not* a straightforward question.

- *Compare your job against other versions of your job (official versions, peers' versions, etc.).* Sometimes, we accept strange or even counterproductive elements of our jobs because we don't have anything to compare them to. Many an expose or even a

Effective

lawsuit is built from this premise: I didn't know it wasn't normal to have to walk the CEO's dog! There's no "right" version of any given job, but comparing notes against anything from how the Department of Labor defines it to how your office neighbor defines it can give you some insight into the most positive and negative features of your particular version.

- *Think about how your job has changed—and depending on why, take the right action.* Many of us reflect thoughtfully on our jobs when we first take them. But then months and years pass, and the job has legitimately shifted, right under our feet. Understanding what has changed, and why, gives us a roadmap to productive action. If your job has mysteriously grown in scope without any compensating factors, time for a conversation with your manager about getting (the right) things off your plate. If your job has changed due to an organizational strategy shift or other organizational change, then the discussion is more about getting the support you need to make it work. And if your job has changed due to technology, you'll want to find ways to play and experiment with that technology—to "be a crow" and have a good time with tools that are, after all, intended to help you.

- *Talk to someone about what your job looks like, today and tomorrow.* All of the introspection in the world will only take you so far. After you've reflected on your job using the different lenses and tools in this chapter, go talk to somebody! Your manager, a mentor, your peers . . . these discussions are what will create action on the back end, getting you support or spurring change to make you more effective. Don't keep your insights to yourself, and don't accept them as gospel, either. Pressure test your thinking and see if you can help get everyone around you working better.

21

The Simple Power of Being Effective

If you're the boss

- *Set up a "what's in my job?" conversation with your direct reports—separate from performance conversations.* A former boss once shared a quote with me: "There are no underperformers—just people in the wrong job." When I was in the corporate world, every performance management season I thought about this quote. As a younger and less experienced manager, I thought this meant people should either get fired or should realize things were not working out and go get new jobs! With the benefit of a few decades of seasoning, and some detailed study of work and jobs, I now realize that "the wrong job" can be one where interpretations of the job vary, or clarity as to what the job is simply does not exist.

- *With that frame in mind, tee up some conversations with your direct reports not about their performance, but about what they believe their jobs to be.* As they say on the Internet, "the results will shock you." You'll identify everything from completely misaligned individual expectations to scary levels of overlap between different people's work/key responsibilities being performed by no one. You might have people out there doing parts of *your* job! Talk about the job, not the person, and get different data—useful data.

If you're the big boss

- *At key organizational moments, sit down and look at leaders' actual jobs—including how those jobs work together (or don't).* We'll get into what you should know about how jobs are supposed to be designed in the next chapter, but for now let me share a dirty little secret I've gleaned from years in organizational consulting: there's a whole set of well-paid, critically important

Effective

leadership roles out there that are just horribly designed. These roles tend to sit a click or two below the C-suite, and carry a lot of strategic weight in the organization. And they contain collections of responsibilities that make absolutely no sense. None.

- *Keep an eye out for jobs that sound amazing, but are ill thought out at the root.* Particularly susceptible to this malady are "transformation" roles, into which are packed a witch's brew of "technology" responsibilities (but often not control over the underlying technology), "influencing" responsibilities ("we expect you to lead people that don't report to you without any levers of actually shifting their actions"), and "strategic" responsibilities (pure hot air, or empty bureaucratic process). Each item is poorly defined or underpowered, and there's no coherence to the combination. As a senior executive, if you can identify even one role like this that's improperly built at the root, you give yourself the opportunity to unstick long-standing challenges. Identify a few roles like this that also don't work well with each other and you can change the organization's whole trajectory. And who knows . . . one of those roles might be your own . . . and you can debug your own working life, too.

23

The Simple Power of Being Effective

Chapter 2

Building Your Effectiveness Architecture to Withstand a Changing World

What does it mean to be effective at work, anyway?

Writer and actor Brett Goldstein rocked the business world in 2021 when he asserted, on Brene Brown's podcast, that "The secret of the Muppets is they're not very good at what they do. Like Kermit's not a great host, Fozzie is not a good comedian, Miss Piggy is not a great . . . None of them are actually good at it, but they f*cking love it . . ."[1]

Goldstein's main point—that you don't have to be perfect to get out there and try, especially surrounded by people who care about you—is a terrific one.

But as a fellow Muppets superfan, I really went down a rabbit hole about his basic assertion.

Are the Muppets bad at their jobs? Is Muppet work substandard work?

I would argue that the picture is more nuanced than Goldstein makes it out to be. Kermit, for instance, repeatedly proves himself a basically effective reporter on Sesame Street; he's just thrown into a disproportionate number of chaotic situations. (A subject we address in Chapter 9!) Animal is a good drummer, but struggles with the lifestyle issues that have challenged drummers across an array of famous bands (including Spinal Tap). Jury's out on the culinary performance of the Swedish Chef or Rizzo, and the other rats-as-chefs in *Muppets Take Manhattan*—we haven't personally tasted their food.

All kidding aside, it's interesting to try to parse out the cultural stories we tell about being effective at work vs. not. The American version of *The Office* has a repeated gag about Michael Scott actually being good at the business of selling paper, as showcased in the episode "The Convention," where he signs up a major supplier even as his boss, Jan, berates him for mismanagement.[2] He's not actually always a terrible manager himself, either. In the "Survivor Man" episode, where Michael runs off to the wilderness, Jim struggles to run the office and realizes that Michael has some chops as a boss, too.[3] In *The Wire*, mastermind Stringer Bell goes to business school to up his game as a drug lord and applies the lessons in real time thoughtfully (and hilariously).[4]

As my Gen Alpha daughter would say, being effective is a whole vibe.

Effectiveness: Getting the Basics Right

Let's ask a really basic question: What has to be true for you to be effective?

Maybe not the "everything" answer that covers 100% of it, but what has to basically be in place for you to be successful? The 80% answer?

To develop something simple and useable, I looked across all the ways organizations, academics, consultants, and other "thought leaders" (you'll never see me use that last term *not* in quotes!) describe work. No surprise: there's a lot of money to be had in figuring this out. Organizational consultancies—like the ones I've worked for— get paid thousands and even millions of dollars to dissect and redissect jobs and work. Companies with enough HR bandwidth pay their own personnel to spend countless hours doing the same. Some use

Effective

approaches that are extremely scientific or data/AI-driven; some just write words on a page, like little job haikus. But both groups seek to paint a clear picture, job by job, of what good looks like.

Examine it all, and you'll see there are many ways to skin a cat—and true to that metaphor, the cat does not emerge from the skinning process super pleased. It's messy out there! Depending who you talk to, the "really important thing" might be skills, competencies, capabilities, tasks, abilities, traits, behaviors, activities, work context, certifications . . . is your head spinning yet? It's Byzantine, and as a former co-worker delightfully once reminded me as I complained about a multi-part proposal we were involved in, complexity did actually hasten the collapse of Byzantium. The term is pejorative for a reason.

Here's another weird thing: none of the categories I just rattled off really capture doing great work in a holistic way—that *je ne sais quoi* of putting it all together. You might call it mojo or X factor. It's critical to find a way to speak about that; it shouldn't be mysterious, and it should be consistent from the most simple-to-describe jobs up to the most complex.

There's another piece, too: how we describe work is often *unhelpful to the individuals doing the work*. When was the last time you read a job description with a straight face? Or sat with a formalized list of skills and ticked off the ones you did and did not have? I'm saying this as someone who has, at several different jobs, opened up the Workday page about her role and just started laughing. In every case the job description was a mixture of absolutely generic statements, some super wishful thinking, and a sprinkling of pure gobbledygook. That wasn't because my employers were somehow writing it wrong—they were writing it in a way that was helpful *to them*. The generic statements, for instance, pertained to the leveling of my role, and the associated compensation. More specificity would have been worse for them—even if I needed it.

27

Building Your Effectiveness Architecture

Introducing the Effectiveness Architecture

So, for the purposes of this book, we're going to use a language and a simple system to describe work *that aims to help the people doing that work be more effective at doing it.*

We'll call this your **Effectiveness Architecture**. Think about a simple two-story house (see Figure 2.1). You have a ground floor and a second floor, each divided into two rooms. Your ground-floor capability is most essential, and your second-floor capability helps you do everything well.

We can use the acronym "KeMPT" to remember what's in the Effectiveness Architecture: instead of your job being unruly—unkempt!—you navigate to a more manageable way of operating, leveraging Knowledge, Methods, People Ability, and Technology Ability.

You can think about what makes you effective in very simple terms:

1. **Knowledge.** You have to know things (*where you start*).

2. **Methods.** You have to have a systematic approach (*what brings it all together*).

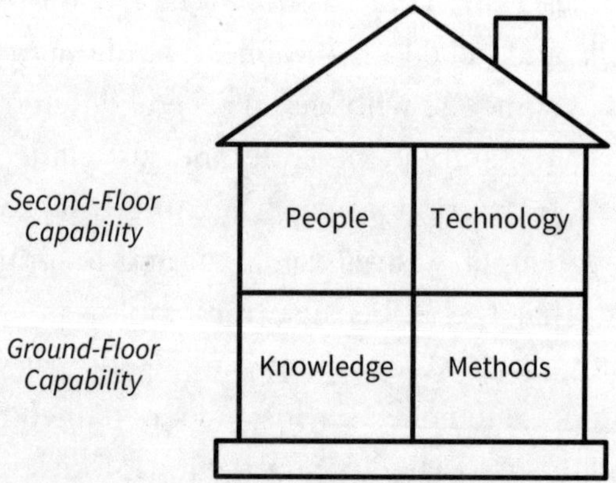

Figure 2.1 Effectiveness Architecture

Effective

3. **People Ability.** You have to be able to work with people (*what helps you go far*).

4. **Technology Ability.** You have to be able to work with technology (*what helps you go quickly*).

Knowing where you are strong in this architecture—understanding your main source of effectiveness—gives you both day-to-day power and importantly, better adaptability as the outside world changes fast. If your strength is Knowledge, you navigate each day differently than someone whose strength is Technology—and your career will also play out differently, calling for you to make different moves. Understanding where you find challenges also gives you good clarity as to how others may perceive you. It's a fine balance between trying to be strong across the whole Effectiveness Architecture and truly leaning into your strength. In general, I recommend doing the latter while paying attention to the former.

Applying the Effectiveness Architecture in the Real World

Now, let's look at the categories of the Effectiveness Architecture against a couple of different jobs: a chemist and a restaurant manager.

You have to know things to do both jobs. The chemist needs to understand everything from the complexity of chemical reactions to the key principles of lab safety; the restaurant manager needs to grasp dealing with difficult customers, food deliveries, and city inspections . . . just for starters. That's foundational, which is why we call knowledge "the base."

As per the cliché, knowing may be half the battle . . . but just half. You can know a ton about your work, but if you can't put it all together in a systematic way that enables you to be effective in the real world, you're sunk. We don't always think about the

Building Your Effectiveness Architecture

methods piece of doing your job, which is why we call it the "secret ingredient"—a huge differentiator between being awesome and just eking it out.

In the case of the chemist, having strong methods might mean being able to put together a series of smart experiments that can run concurrently in a high-functioning lab. Doing this systematically requires a sharp sense of balance, prioritization, and indeed systems thinking—knowing how all the moving parts work together. For the restaurant manager, having strong methods means both having a well-thought-out way to navigate the average night—keeping customers happy and staff sane—but also the not-so-average night. Strong methods encompass black swan events and worst-case scenarios: what to do if there's an explosion in the lab, a critic visiting the restaurant, and so on.

And in both jobs, of course, you have to be able to deal with people, and you have to be able to deal with technology. The chemist might handle scientific colleagues or reviewers; the restaurant manager might handle waiters, cooks, and that demanding bunch of foodies at Table 5. Technology? Anything from pipettes to complex spectrometers for the chemist; cash registers, point-of-sale systems, and even stoves for the restaurant manager. We consider people "the catalyst" because you generally need to interact with people to get anything going; we consider technology "the accelerant" because it helps you get everything done faster.

Intuitively, one might think that there are some jobs that are basically solitary or technology-free. Nope! Our friends at O*Net, the US Government job database, actually ranked jobs by "social orientation": "Job requires preferring to work with others rather than alone, and being personally connected with others on the job." Even the most solitary job they ranked—Poets, Lyricists and Creative Writers—gets 18 points out of 100 available. There's no avoiding people![5]

Effective

Similarly, there's no avoiding technology. Remember those crows from Chapter 1 using sticks? A stick is technology in that instance. Anything non-human you use to get your job done is technology— it doesn't have to be advanced AI or even computer-based. Pick strawberries into a basket, and the basket is technology. All jobs are technology-enabled, it just works differently for different roles.

The Effectiveness Architecture is purposefully simple because we're going to use it in different ways to look at different areas of complexity. We'll be using this framework for the rest of the book to understand both how you can tackle some energizing challenges (e.g., a world of rapid technological evolution) as well as some exhausting ones (e.g., chaotic workplaces).

The Weird But Powerful Truth About Effectiveness and Change

Let me share a weird fact from my own career: none of the jobs I've done in the last 20 years still exist.

You know how they say "the common factor in all of your bad relationships is you?" There's definitely a potential theory that my own performance in these jobs was so terrible, so shambolic, that I actually destroyed organizations' appetite for any role that I touched. "We saw how Melissa did that work and the only way to prevent that going forward is for the role to go away entirely."

Was I so bad at all of these jobs that I actually *killed them*?

I love this theory so much. I could put lox and capers on it and eat it for breakfast.

But the truth—like most truths—is more boring and complicated. In some cases the organization exited the business entirely. Or they exited and got back in years later (I say this with a loving side-eye toward a former employer). More often, I took on leadership roles in emerging lines of business where the organizational clay was still wet. In those cases, the company reformed the job meaningfully using the learning from my tenure—putting the organizational Lego together in very different combinations.

It's been a wild ride for me. But pull the lens out a bit and that's all of us. Whether you've danced from organization to organization or dug in at a place you love, change is the dragon chasing us all.

Raise your hand if *none* of these things has ever happened to you: Your organization was bought or merged. Your organization bought another organization. New technology was introduced at work. Old technology was retired. Your manager changed. Your direct reports changed. The CEO changed. You got promoted. You were made redundant. Someone else was made redundant and you got their responsibilities. Your product or service mix changed. There was a "reorganization." There was another "reorganization." There were so many "reorganizations" that you stopped paying attention. A "reorganization" returned things back to the original state, but you didn't have the heart to tell anyone.

And so on. The reality is: work does not stand still, and especially not during moments of rapid technological change like the one we're living through.

Here's the interesting paradox—and what ultimately got me personally from sometimes painful transitions into often energizing plateaus: *The better you know the core of what makes you good at your work, the easier it is to deal with change in the work you do, whether you choose that change or not.*

This truth saved my (professional) life. And it'll save yours—whether you want to ever change what you do, or whether you want to have a multi-decade career doing the same thing, as the landscape of work changes fast underneath you. These days it takes a lot of flexibility and ingenuity to either stay roughly in the same place or swing like a

Effective

cheerful bonobo around the "career jungle gym." What enables all that pivoting is a *solid core of understanding what makes you great at work and where you experience challenges*.

An important thing to note before we proceed: while every part of the model is important, *the point is not that you have to be equally good at all four parts*. We all struggle to allocate limited time and finite energy. And "pobody's nerfect." No matter how much of an "insecure overachiever" you are, it's a waste of life spirit to chase perfection—and a quixotic quest anyway. You're not gonna get there. What we're going for here is the self-awareness that will help you up your game, advocate for yourself, and also understand how others perceive you, in service of better interactions.

Fully optional: if you want to really dive into what might be your areas of strength and challenge, there's a 40-question quiz in the Appendix. This will give you some detailed insight into your strengths and challenges across the Effectiveness Architecture.

But if you're not up for a quiz, read on! You will be able to intuit where you stand based on the descriptions below, too.

For each piece of the framework, we'll look at the same things:

1. What is it?

2. How do you know if this is an area of strength for you?

3. How can you better think about what you're dealing with in this area today?

4. What does disruption look like in this area?

When you've worked through each area, you'll be equipped with a neat "cheat sheet" as to what makes you effective at work—including a roadmap as to how you can develop further and constructively get ahead of disruption.

Building Your Effectiveness Architecture

As Chapter 2 Draws to a Close . . .

Before we get into the details of effectiveness across Knowledge, Methods, People, and Technology in Chapters 3 and 4, here are a few actions to consider.

For everyone

- *Reflect on how you describe your own effectiveness. What specific words do you use?* If you get one thing out of Chapters 3 and 4, it should be a good understanding of which of the components of the Effectiveness Architecture—Knowledge, Methods, People, or Technology—represent your true area of strength. But whether you get there through reading and reflection or taking the quiz in the Appendix, you'll need a baseline of self-knowledge first. So, consider: How do you talk about your own effectiveness today? What *language* do you use? For example, I have a treasured former colleague who always says his strength is as an operator. Within a large, complex organization, he perceives himself (correctly!) as working well with an array of technology, processes, and people to straightforwardly get stuff done. That language—"I see myself as an operator"—is a tell that his strength is Methods. So, before we go deep on the components of the Effectiveness Architecture, see if your self-description might hold some clues as to your particular area of strength.

If you're the boss

- *Think about how you describe your team's effectiveness, and what decisions you make on that basis.* Just like you have a working image of yourself and your own effectiveness, if you have a team you definitely have a working view of what their

Effective

collective strength (or strengths) are within the Effectiveness Architecture. Do you see your team as experts (*Knowledge*), operators (*Methods*), people-people (no surprise—*People!*), or technology whizzes (*Technology*)? Think about what decisions you then make on that basis. For example, do you leave new hire orientations largely unstructured because you believe your team has such a strength in the People dimension that they will handle this process brilliantly without a lot of guidance? You'll also want to consider whether the way you characterize your team is accurate to your team today, and whether it is accurate to all team members. For example, your team may be mostly Methods folks, but if there's a Knowledge person embedded in there that you're not fully considering, you may be missing out on their full capability and contribution.

If you're the big boss

- *As you read the next two chapters, reflect on how your business strategy relates to the collective effectiveness strengths of your workforce.* Pretty much every organization in the world has a combination of folks strong in Knowledge, Methods, People, and Technology. Depending on your business strategy, of course, the proportions may be very different. As you look in depth at the components of the Effectiveness Architecture across the next couple of chapters, it's worth reflecting on the relationship between your business strategy, the actual areas of effectiveness of your workforce, and any preconceived notions or preferences that may be shaping a mismatch. For example, certain industries need a lot of certain folks, just by the very nature of their business. Manufacturing would be sunk without a lot of Methods people, and the search industry can't function without a lot of People-people. But these overall

Building Your Effectiveness Architecture

needs sometimes create too strong of a preference—and you end up with, let's say, people with an effectiveness strength in Methods in roles that would be better served by someone with a strength in Technology. Reproduce that across an entire organization, and you can veer far off the strategic track.

We've taken a first look at the overall Effectiveness Architecture. Now let's get specific, starting with the foundational stuff—the first floor: Knowledge and Methods.

Chapter 3

The Ground Floor of Your Effectiveness Architecture: Knowledge and Methods

There's an exchange in the venerable 1980s classic movie *The Breakfast Club* that perfectly encapsulates the themes of this chapter. Brian ("the brain") and Bender ("the criminal") are arguing about Brian's otherwise perfect academic record being marred by an F in shop class.

Brian defends himself, stating "Did you know without trigonometry, there'd be no engineering?"

Bender fires back instantly: "Without lamps, there'd be no light."[1]

Those two ways of thinking are what this chapter is about. The Knowledge portion of the Effectiveness Architecture is all about things like understanding the trigonometry that drives the engineering that underlies electricity; the Methods part is all about constructing lamps that actually turn on.

You need both personally; teams need both; organizations need both.

Let's start by looking at Knowledge.

Knowledge: The Base

I want you to close your eyes and imagine a TV show—a procedural, specifically. Procedurals "focus on professional problem-solving in fields like law enforcement, medicine, and law."[2] If you've ever watched *House, ER, Gray's Anatomy, Law and Order* (any of them!), *Matlock*, *Suits*, *LA Law* (I'm dating myself with that last one!), you've seen a procedural. Same format every week: detectives solve crimes, doctors diagnose and treat patients, lawyers argue cases.

This procedural is a little different, though. It's about people doing a particular job, who actually don't know a thing about that job. If it's a medical procedural, the doctors lack knowledge of basic anatomy; for a law procedural, the lawyers don't understand the basic criminal code; for a crime-solving procedural, the detectives are unaware of the basic rules of evidence.

As a result, the people in it stink at their basic work. They're completely ineffective. Everything goes wrong as a result: patients die, crimes go unsolved, innocent people go to jail. This happens week after week.

If you're a total nihilist, you might think this is amusing. (You might also dress in all black and own ferrets, or maybe I've watched *The Big Lebowski* too many times?)

For the rest of us, this show would become unwatchable pretty quickly. It would be unbelievably frustrating to watch people bungle their jobs because they literally didn't know what they were doing.

That's why Knowledge is a core part of our Effectiveness Architecture. For every kind of work, you have to know *something*.

To understand the concept of Knowledge as a core part of your work performance, you can also think about a common phrase you might hear on TV shows about spies, the government, or the military: "need to know basis." In highly sensitive environments, knowledge is parceled out very carefully: you are allowed to know just what you need to know to do your job—nothing more.

So, here's a fun thought experiment: let's say your (probably not very secret) job allocated information to you on a "need to know" basis. What would you actually need to know? That's the

Effective

Knowledge component of the model in a nutshell. It's not all the fun facts you might annoy Frank down the hall by reciting during lunch breaks; it's what you actually *must* know to get your work done.

Let me be clear here: Knowledge is *not* supposed to be static. Quite the opposite, part of really knowing things is knowing when and how things change, and having great mental systems in place to learn more and build your understanding further.

Knowledge: How Do I Know If This Is My Area of Strength?

Identifying which part of the model you're strongest at can be tricky. We get a lot of messaging about what we're good at—from our childhoods, our friends, our organizations . . . even the culture of the countries we live in.

So, to identify your area of strength, we're going to look for some observable hallmarks.

In other words: if you're strong in this particular area, what do you either *see yourself doing* or *see happening*? Observability is the key—if you can't see it, it may not be happening.

Here are some observable hallmarks of Knowledge being your area of strength:

- People often come to you with questions, especially when things are changing fast. They might make jokes about you being better than Google/AI!

- You get pulled into onboarding processes to talk about a particular area or areas.

- Someone has called you a subject matter expert or "thought leader" (I know we hate that second term, but it is a "tell" for being strong in Knowledge).

The Ground Floor of Your Effectiveness Architecture

- You're always taking classes—online, at universities, wherever. You might have multiple degrees, or just be a lifelong learner in other ways.

- Your favorite social media platform is Reddit.

Knowledge: What Am I Grappling with Today?

There are going to be two types of knowledge to think about—and both are important. If you've ever geeked out on knowledge management—and I understand this will be a small subset of readers—you know that often, knowledge at work is "tacit," or hidden from the knowledge holder's view. You know something, but you don't know that you know it. This is less common in fields like medicine or accounting, where a good deal of formal training is mandated, and more common in fields like construction or consulting, where you learn almost entirely by doing. Concepts learned outside the classroom seep into your brain like rainwater into soil. Just like the plants that then spring up, your activities at work take hold thanks to nourishment that's not strictly visible—tacit knowledge.

Let's take a minute and start to map out what you know that helps you do your job. In doing so, we're going to set a roadmap for constantly doing better at the Knowledge component. This may feel a bit weird or silly if you consider yourself an expert, hold a senior executive role, or have been doing the same thing for decades. But bear with me: do this part right and it'll give you a great path to what you should be learning to stay on top of a fast-moving environment, even as a star in your field. As a bonus, mapping your tacit knowledge should give you a bit of an emotional boost. You're taking a minute and giving yourself credit for things you haven't before.

So, divide a sheet of paper into four sections. Going side to side, label one side "explicit knowledge" and the other side "tacit

Effective

knowledge." Then, going top to bottom, label the top of the page "I know it" and the bottom of the page "I don't know it."

Now, fill out each of the four quadrants with a few quick bullet points—no more than five. Important while doing this: *practice self-compassion*. You're doing an inventory with a purpose, so don't beat up on yourself as you think through where you may have gaps. Here's how to think about each one:

- *Explicit knowledge/"I know it."* This is the easiest quadrant to fill out. What well-documented knowledge areas help you do your job well?

- *Explicit knowledge/"I don't know it."* Many answers here will relate to fast-moving technological change. Virtually all of us, for instance, could get better at our jobs by learning to leverage AI better. As you progress in your career, other gaps in explicit knowledge emerge at lifecycle points, too. If you're managing a budget for the first time, for instance, that's a great knowledge gap to identify and consciously address.

- *Tacit knowledge/"I know it."* This is an opportunity to give yourself a bit of a pat on the back. What do you know that no one would write down in a book, but definitely helps you perform better? For instance, some leaders have a great grasp on how to manage 1:1s with their direct reports so that they're neither micromanaging nor ignoring folks.

- *Tacit knowledge/"I don't know it."* This is the quadrant that demands the most introspection. What "secret sauce" are you missing? Think about people you really look up to who do similar work or a more advanced version of your work—what are they amazing at that's not a book-learning sort of skill? Capability relating to emotional intelligence or smooth communications often falls into this category—often, doing your job at a higher

41

The Ground Floor of Your Effectiveness Architecture

level just means doing the same basic work, but speaking about it in a way that lands more effectively. Press yourself mentally here: to some extent, you're looking for "unknown unknowns."

You now have a practical map of your work-related knowledge. We'll use this map throughout the book, but here are a few things you can do with it immediately:

1. *Create a learning roadmap for yourself.* Seeing where you've identified gaps in your current knowledge, how will you go and acquire that understanding? The answer could be anything from "YouTube" to "talking to Billy down the hall." Making a simple list of what knowledge you want to go after, and how you'll get there, can really speed up your continuous learning journey.

2. *Talk to your manager about opportunities that will help you grow.* The quadrant marked Tacit Knowledge/"I don't know it" can serve as the touchpoint for a great conversation about what on-the-job learning opportunities you should be seeking—within the context of your current role, in lateral projects in different areas, in stretch projects, or in your next role entirely. Tacit knowledge is the stuff you can't get from YouTube.

3. *Identify areas where you want to mentor or teach.* All that stuff in the "I know it" column is wonderful fodder for everything from informal mentoring to formal teaching in academic settings.

Knowledge: What Does Disruption Look Like?

Every day, it seems, I see some ding-dong on LinkedIn trumpeting the same message: Knowledge is dead! Now that we have AI, you

Effective

don't need to know anything. Sit back, wipe your brain, and let the machines take over.

Sigh. As much as I sometimes fear we are living in the remarkably knowledge-free world portrayed in the 2006 no-longer-a-satire *Idiocracy*,[2] the reality is that regardless of your age, in your lifetime you've already lived through dramatic technological disruption. And despite the advent of things like the Internet collecting most human knowledge, and technologies like AI and search engines helping us access it better, we all seem, day-to-day, to be on the hook for knowing stuff.

In fact, when it comes to Knowledge getting disrupted by technology, we actually have a picture-perfect case study delivered to us by the city of London. To get people from point A to point B in a city that makes my hometown, New York City, look small and simply organized, London cab drivers have historically had to pass a detailed test on a body of knowledge about where different streets and landmarks are. They call this body of knowledge . . . drum roll please . . . *The Knowledge.*

The Knowledge was officially introduced in 1865 because people were sick of their cab drivers getting lost—perfectly showcasing the relationship between knowledge and job performance! "Here, please memorize these facts and for the love of God, stop screwing up."[3] Today, it encompasses more than 26,000 streets and locations. If the thought of memorizing 26,000 of anything blows your mind, think about this: neuroscience research actually shows "changes in the grey matter density of [London cab drivers'] hippocampuses."[4] Memorizing that many things doesn't just make your customers happier—it makes your own brain grow.

It's all written down in a book called *The Blue Book*, which is pink.[5] And the test on The Knowledge is considered by some to be the hardest exam in the world—taking many folks multiple years to pass, and involving driving around London on a motorbike,

The Ground Floor of Your Effectiveness Architecture

memorizing little urban details that could change at a moment's notice.[6]

And then GPS appeared on the scene: meaning everyone had a little advisor inside their car telling them what turn to take when.

Lights out for The Knowledge, right?

In fact, understanding how The Knowledge has—and has not—gotten disrupted by technological advances is a fabulous guide to what disruption of the Knowledge part of our model really looks like in practice. There are some good lessons for us all about how to be strategic about not losing the value of what we know.

Let's start with a brute-force question: Did the introduction of GPS reduce the number of black cabs in London?

Yes—but importantly, not immediately and not on its own.

Yahoo and Google announced consumer GPS products in 2004 and 2005, respectively; importantly for the transportation use case, these products were available on smartphones in 2007.[7] You'd think the black cab industry would be whacked immediately. Instead, from 2007 to 2012, the number of black cabs actually *grows*, from 21,792 to 23,099.[8]

GPS didn't disrupt The Knowledge. A single technology is generally not enough to overwhelm deep human expertise.

But what started to happen in 2011 *does* cause real disruption, and as of 2025, London has gone from 23,000 black cabs to more like 14,000.[9]

In 2011, Uber showed up.[10] Uber, and other ridesharing companies, don't rely just on GPS. Uber has more than 3,000 patents globally, across everything from payments to maps to general algorithmic management.[11] It's not one technology challenging the supremacy of The Knowledge as a way of understanding the complex roadscape of London; it's a sophisticated set of companies, leveraging an array of coordinated technologies, regulatorily challenging the whole black cab system, including rates, licenses, and, as of recently, whether drivers are required at all.[12]

44

Effective

What does the story of The Knowledge mean then for humans worried about the Knowledge portion of how they do their jobs being disrupted? There are a few key lessons to this story:

1. *Don't sweat a single technology.* If you'd panicked and abandoned your job as a London cabbie the second GPS hit smartphones, you would have missed some really productive years when your profession was actually still growing.

2. *Do pay attention to the disruption actual companies are producing.* Ignoring the rise of Uber, in contrast, would have been an unwise move for London cabbies. Uber operated out of a long-held playbook—leveraging multiple technologies but also changing the landscape (in this case, regulatory) to suit its business goals. This is not a new playbook: think of the Ford and Packard Motor Companies—plus Goodyear Tires—both building paved roads themselves and advocating for government construction of the same.[13] Companies armed with a transformative worldview in addition to new technology can and will do a lot to bring that future into existence. And if you were a horse-and-buggy driver in the early 20th century . . . your job *was* eventually affected.

3. *Don't go into short-term panic mode—you have some time, so use it to scenario plan.* There's a ton of rhetoric out there about how fast things are changing, and how quickly you need to adapt—especially to changes in Knowledge. Don't slow down your continuous learning . . . but don't freak out either. In the London black cab example, drivers had five or so years before things started to really shift—and even today, 18 years after the advent of GPS, their jobs are just reduced in number, not eliminated. Folks might argue that the pace of technological adoption has speeded up—and they'd be right. Remember, though, first, it's not the technology

The Ground Floor of Your Effectiveness Architecture

that's disruptive, it's a company or companies deploying it as part of their arsenal. Second, even if we speed up from the black cab case study timelines, that still gives you a good chunk of time to prepare for all the ways your job might change. Use it wisely!

Methods: The Secret Ingredient

Have you ever watched someone who was good at their job, and marveled at it?

A flight attendant deftly wrangling hundreds of people to board a flight. A teacher shepherding unruly third graders around the Natural History Museum with grace. A journalist shaping a story so it reads like a tiny novel.

What's often impressive isn't how they do one thing, one particular task—it's how they do all the things, in the right sequence, all at once, elegant and effortless. They bring everything together in a flow that's at once calming and energizing.

You're not witnessing magic. You're watching someone with some methods.

Ooh, you might be thinking, teach me these magical methods. I wish it was that simple! What's actually helpful is to have *a* system, *any* system—wholly of your own invention, borrowed from or learned from someone else, or anywhere in between. You need a way of looking at your working world in totality, and a way of navigating it that basically tells you how to relate tasks to each other and how to spend your time. Good methods accomplish what's called "sensemaking": "coming up with a plausible understanding—a map—of a shifting world."[14] They put all of the disparate elements together and give you what to do next.

The key, after all, is the end result. Noted cybernetician Stafford Beer put it beautifully: "the purpose of a system is what it does,"

Effective

often abbreviated as "posiwid." If your methods spit out the wrong thing, they represent the wrong system. (Side note: What job is cooler than "cybernetician?")

Richard Nixon, in the 1960 presidential race, offers a great example of a decent-sounding method that didn't work. Nixon pledged to visit all 50 states, which sounded like a wonderful way to embrace the entire country. He was acknowledging that different states had very different needs; that voters needed to connect to the candidate in person; and that all the states should be heard. He had an automatic roadmap of where to visit: everywhere. There was a system in place.

It looked like a strong system, a good set of methods. But let's come back to "posiwid." What did this system do? It *exhausted* Nixon. In a tight race where Nixon actually spent several days in hospital after developing septic arthritis from a knee injury, the excess travel time visiting all 50 states mandated added to his woes and ended up making him more visibly tired, and less appealing of a candidate. In perhaps the first great television campaign, against a highly appearance-conscious opponent (JFK), looking awake mattered. Nixon's system seemed well thought out, but it didn't deliver.[15]

Good Methods enable you to get stuff done, even when things get weird. They don't have to be set in stone—and in fact, they shouldn't be. Being amazing at Methods means having a well-locked-down array of *stuff to try*. Think and work like a designer, as NYU Initiative on Purpose and Flourishing Associate Director Dustin Liu puts it eloquently:

> *I think what designers do really well is even if something doesn't work out, they know where to start again. Moving through ambiguity is to try and try again and to learn from those trials. What does it mean to test something so that you have enough data to move forward and iterate?*

Let's pause and admire that phrase: "they know where to start again." This is the essence of Methods—that wonderful balance between "I have real strategies" and "I know what to do when a particular strategy fails."

Nail that dichotomy and move the world.

Methods: How Do I Know If This Is My Area of Strength?

Folks who are great at Methods are often the unsung heroes and heroines of the world of effectiveness. They're not lauded as geniuses, like folks who are strong at Knowledge; they're not the cool kids, like folks who are great with Technology; and they're not the popular kids, like folks who excel at dealing with People. Sometimes they even fade into the background, because their gifts of making systems operate well can be undetectable when done well.

Here are some observable hallmarks of Methods being your area of strength:

- You are often asked to train other people at work.

- People ask "how you do it all."

- You get pulled into onboarding processes as an overall guide to a new joiner.

- You're pulled into messy work situations to clean them up.

- You're given stretch opportunities well afield of your original area of expertise.

Methods: What Am I Grappling with Today?

So, let's look at *your* methods for doing your job—what they are today, and what they could be. If you've ever told a co-worker "there's a method to my madness"—now's the time to unveil it! Because we're at the heart big Stafford Beer fans, we'll derive these elements from systems thinking—albeit in a highly simplified form.

Grab a sheet of paper and label it with these headings, or use your workbook to look at and fill in the following categories:

1. *Underlying worldview.* What do you think you're meant to be accomplishing, and how are you accomplishing it? This might be a tight summary of the job description you worked up in Chapter 1, or it might be a bigger-picture philosophical statement. In the movie *Barbie*, Ken offers just this sort of statement: "You know surfer is not even my job . . . And it is not lifeguard, which is a common misconception . . . Because actually my job . . . it's just beach."[16] Ken has captured his underlying worldview about his job with great clarity. Surfers ride waves; lifeguards save people. But his job is just beach—hanging out in the sun and looking cool. That's a coherent worldview—it gives him what he's meant to be doing and how to do it. What is yours?

2. *Components of your job and how they relate.* Systems thinking concerns itself to a great degree with parts, wholes, and how they interact with each other. Accordingly, let's look at a simple question: what are the different pieces of your job, and how do they relate to each other? There's no "right" way to do this. The pieces might be different customer groups (B2B customer vs. B2C), different kinds of activities (being in meetings vs. solo writing), even different parts of the average day (dinner rush vs. quiet breakfast service). You can write a few paragraphs on how these relate to each other and what you then do as a result. ("Some of my customers are angrier than others; I handle those calls at the beginning of the day when I have more energy.") Or, if you're a more visual person, you can create a diagram of how the different pieces play off each other—use boxes and arrows if that resonates better. The key

49

to this piece is to create a reasonable summary of how you do
your job from a systematic perspective. If you can look at it
and say "yes, that's my job and that's a decent capture on how
it all works together," you've nailed this piece.

3. *Limits of your job.* Any good cybernetician (love to type that!)
will tell you that a proper system has boundaries. What are the
limits of your job? What does your job *not* do? (You may have
identified some of this in Chapter 1.) Believe it or not, the
limits of your job are part of your methods; knowing what you
don't do helps you get what you *do* do, done better. These
limits can be frustrating too—for instance, many executives
tear their hair out over not fully owning compensation decisions for their team. For them, the boundary of their system
feels too small to be effective. What are the boundaries of
your system—good and bad?

4. *What you do when things go wrong (or just change meaningfully).* Finally, strong systems are adaptable. What in
your methods helps you adapt? Everything else you've written in steps 1–3 might be about the best-case-scenario—
what about when things go fully bonkers? What about when
things shift in real time? Do you have approaches that you
use over and over? For example, many executives have a
strong sense of what meetings they can miss when their day
gets overloaded, and which ones can't be missed without
serious consequences. It's a great example of an adaptive
method. You may have 100, or you may have 5. Again—no
"right" answer.

You've just captured your "secret ingredient"—the method underlying how you think about, and do, your job. This is what a task-by-
task view, or a list of skills, isn't going to tell you: how you put it all

Effective

together. We'll use this throughout the book, but for now here are a few things you can do with this write-up (and maybe a drawing):

1. *Look for—and take action on—"a-ha"s.* What stands out to you is what's important, and deserves not just reflection but follow-up action. Most of us never sit down and think through *how* we do our job . . . which is what you've just done. Take a step back. What stands out to you? What seems compelling? What worries you? Do you see areas where it might make sense to reflect a bit further? For instance, do you have a lot of strategies for when things go wrong, but not a lot on how you organize your job in the first place? Did you struggle to write down the boundaries of your job because you're frankly not sure where your job ends and the next person's job begins? Did you define your job in an exciting way you've never thought about it before? Look at what jumps out, for better or for worse, and start to strategize about what you're going to do as a result.

2. *Pressure test how adaptive your methods are.* When you captured what you do when things change or go wrong, you were probably picturing moments from the past, when something did change or go wrong. Do a thought experiment: What if the change was a thousand times more extreme? What if things went terribly, terribly wrong? You can pressure test how adaptive your methods are against a stock set of scenarios. Think about how you might systematically do your job differently against such varied scenarios as your company being acquired (or your division being spun out), your manager changing, a catastrophic event/natural disaster, large-scale layoffs in your company, and so on. By pushing the scenarios to the extreme, you get a great read on whether your methods can flex well enough day to day. If you find

The Ground Floor of Your Effectiveness Architecture

areas where your thinking currently seems inadequate, it's worth a bit of further thought.

Methods: What Does Disruption Look Like?

Are Methods, as an area of strength, under pressure as work evolves? Yes and no. On the yes side, the escalation of chaotic, intensified work (which we'll dig into in Chapters 8 and 5, respectively) is generically putting a ton of pressure on how we systematically approach each day. That said, the core of many folks' Methods—techniques like prioritization—will still serve them well even as work gets harder in some ways.

For example, the air traffic controller (ATC) we'll spend more time with in Chapter 5, Anthony Tisdall, explains that ATCs always prioritize landings over takeoffs. Why? A landing plane is in a vulnerable position; it's in the air. A plane taking off is on the ground; while it's not terrific for it to just sit there, it's perfectly safe doing so. Unless the fundamental nature of how a plane flies changes, any incremental change to technology, process, the scale of airports, and so on won't change this basic prioritization.

You always have to deal with the planes in the air first.

As Chapter 3 Draws to a Close . . .

For everyone

- *Consider your strengths and challenges in Knowledge and Methods—and reflect on how the two interact.* People with incredible strength in Methods often effectively compensate for Knowledge challenges by systematically accessing the Knowledge strength of others. This is a valid approach! Similarly, folks who are strong in Knowledge but not in Methods often work their way into roles that are simply more Knowledge

Effective

dependent—so-called subject matter experts. Also valid! Understanding how you balance the two areas gives you good strategies to manage whatever your particular combination of strengths and challenges is.

If you're the boss

- *Ask yourself two simple questions: What is my team's Knowledge? What are my team's Methods?* If you can't answer these easily, talk to your team. If you get the answer and it's unsatisfying, map out ways to address it. Knowledge will be some combination of formal training and on-the-job work to build learning; Methods, in contrast, will come from a conscious discussion of how things get done today—and how they *should* get done tomorrow. This is a fruitful discussion and one many, many teams fail to ever have.

If you're the big boss

- *Ask yourself a different question: Are we a Knowledge or a Methods organization?* Apple is a good example of a Knowledge organization—there's an understanding of a deep language of design that flows through every single thing they do. Amazon, in contrast, is a Methods organization: their success is always predicated on doing things in a particular way that Amazon has worked out. Pre-breakup GE—with "the GE way"—was a Methods organization.

- *Once you've answered that question, reflect on the strengths and challenges that come with that identity.* If you're a Knowledge organization, are you leaning in on your organization's Knowledge enough? (Imagine if only half of Apple products looked like Apple products . . .) Are there limits to your

The Ground Floor of Your Effectiveness Architecture

Knowledge construct that you should acknowledge and deal with? (Think of 1950s Ford overdoing it on knowledge of the customer and creating the market-research-based Edsel, which no customer actually liked.) If you're a Methods organization, same question—are you applying those Methods deeply enough? And do you have a mechanism to hear the voices for people who might "build a better mousetrap"—and come up with a superior method for doing something?

Congratulations by the way: you're halfway through the Effectiveness Architecture. You've covered the ground floor. In the next chapter, let's go on to the second floor—to two things that might really help or hinder you.

People and Technology.

Buckle up.

Chapter 4

The Second Floor of Your Effectiveness Architecture: People and Technology

The two things that help you most at work—and drive you the craziest—aren't anything new.

Working with people? Working with technology? Folks were doing that back in the Pleistocene epoch.

Consider early Homo Sapiens hunting a deer. They're using spears constructed from sticks and jagged rocks[1]—technology—and they're working as a group with differently articulated roles—collaboration among people.[2]

Intriguingly, humans are actually built to collaborate: we're one of the few species that have uniformly white sclera (literally, the white of the eye). Having a white sclera allows you to signal where you're looking to someone else without making a sound—a critical skill during a multi-person hunt.[3] We're designed to achieve better outcomes by working together.

Tools and collaboration kept us alive back then, and they sustain us now.

Just because something is vital, though, doesn't mean it's easy or straightforward. In this chapter we'll explore what it means to have strengths in the People and Technology areas of our Effectiveness Architecture—but also what's tough, or prone to disruption, in each.

Let's start with People. With my white sclera, I'm silently signaling you to look that way!

People: The Catalyst

One in seven people told us that their co-workers were driving them berserk.

Let me back up.

In April 2025, in conjunction with a former co-worker of mine, Patrick Hyland, PhD (who did not drive me berserk!) and hosted by the Remesh platform, my company Anthrome Insight conducted a 1,000-person study on work intensification—a topic we'll explore in detail in Chapter 5, leveraging this wonderful study data.[4]

As part of this study, we asked people on an open-ended basis what was causing them to feel overwhelmed. We got lots of different responses, but a whole cluster of them stood out to me. Some 14% of folks—one in seven respondents—felt exhausted not by their bosses or by the work itself, but by dealing with the people around them: everything from team infighting to fixing co-workers' mistakes to people just acting like jerks.

Sigh. Working with people is tough. As per the O*Net data we looked at earlier, even if you're a poet (or a photonics engineer, or a judicial law clerk—the other two jobs with the lowest social orientation ranking), there's no avoiding those pesky human interactions.

People: How Do I Know If This Is My Area of Strength?

But what does it mean to be *good* at working with people?

This is kind of a weird question, so I'm going to start with what it's *not*. And there are a couple of flavors here.

On the one hand, being good at working with people isn't all sunshine and roses. It doesn't mean being the best-loved person on the team, or being the person whose shoulder everyone cries on (or who has the office they cry in—absolutely me at a prior job). It's not being charming and lovely and, if anyone remembers this phrase from report card days, "a pleasure to have in class."

This is a book about effectiveness. You can be an absolute dear, just the nicest person, and be perfectly ineffective at achieving any sort of results.

Conversely, though, being good at working with people does not mean being a pushy jerk. Getting people to do what you want by "any means necessary" also does not qualify as an effective way of dealing with your co-workers. This remains, to my surprise and horror, a point under debate. I had honestly hoped that Bob Sutton's seminal work, *The No Asshole Rule*, had settled the issue once and for all about the economic costs of verbally body-slamming your colleagues.[5] Perhaps my keeping a copy of Sutton's book on my desk and waving it at people on video calls isn't doing the trick? (Just in case it's working, I'm going to keep doing that.)

I have reflected a lot on this balancing act between kindness and forcefulness, and considered a number of well-respected behavioral models from academia and the business world. Here's where I've landed in terms of a few key behaviors that make you good at working with people:

- *Clear two-way communications.* Can you get people to understand what you mean, and can you listen to and grasp what they mean? This sounds simple but can be devilishly hard, especially in environments that are chaotic, emotional, intensified . . . we'll get more into that in Chapters 6, 7, and 9. The listening side is particularly critical, and as NYU Initiative on Purpose and Flourishing Associate Director Dustin Liu notes, in short supply in a loud world: "The most important people skill of our time right now which is actually just deep listening . . . being fully present, suspending judgment, engaging in dialogue, understanding what someone is saying when they're not actually saying it." UVA professor Jim Detert zeroes in on this gap too: "Talk less and listen more. Every business school has a communications course,

The Second Floor of Your Effectiveness Architecture

but how many great books are in the curriculum of business schools on how to be a good listener? And in the deeply divisive, polarized world we live in we had better learn how to listen . . ."

- *Ability to influence others' actions.* For this one, let's talk about an explicit guardrail. There's a Dark Triad trait, Machiavellianism, which entails treating people as objects to be manipulated—a means to an end.[6] Getting people to do what you want in that way is neither effective nor ethical. The right version of this behavior is the ability to constructively persuade folks to help you—to enlist their support in a way that genuinely benefits them too.

- *Versatility, curiosity, and openness.* As the saying goes, "it takes all types to make a world"—and folks who are really good with people are good with all of them. This often plays out vividly when you watch folks work globally. Every time I speak to my friend Vagesh Dave, CIO at the highly global construction firm McDermott International, he regales me with tales of working with folks all over the world. What I love about these conversations is the level of detail Vagesh shares about working practices in different countries—why it's important to have a movie theater near the office in India, how prayer integrates into the working day in Indonesia, how generations are clashing in the American workplace. He's curious about how folks' approaches and norms differ, and observes them closely. This is a crucial people skill.

- *Boundaries and balance.* Sometimes, being good with people means not letting them get into your head. People who deal effectively with others at work neatly balance an empathic attitude with a clear sense of when to not let others' emotions in—especially "loud" negative emotions. (More on this in Chapter 7 . . .)

That's just four things, but it's quite a lot to handle some days. People are tough!

On that front, I'm often reminded of a story from my long-ago sustainability consulting days. A team of us were trying to convince a consortium of farmers to install methane digesters to earn carbon credits. If you have a weak stomach, please skip this description of methane digesters: they're giant machines that you throw cow poop into, and by capturing the resulting methane emissions rather than letting them flow into the atmosphere, under some financial and regulatory regimes you can earn carbon credits and make money.

We'd run the numbers and they looked great: the earnings from carbon credits far outweighed the cost of installing the digesters. The cow poop, of course, was free. Fabulous economics! But the farmers remained skeptical: they kept muttering that it wouldn't work. Operationally, the digesters just wouldn't capture the gas in the way that was intended. I pressed and pressed for why, and finally one farmer said: "Because it's biology, not physics."

This quote blew my mind. What he meant was that the methane digesters existed in a far messier, more uncertain world than the perfect action-and-reaction world of the Excel spreadsheets we were using.

1. He was right.

And

2. This is a really helpful way to think about people in organizations! "Biology, not physics." When it comes to human beings, assume a whole lot of messiness, and you're more likely to understand the situation better and make better decisions as a result.

The Second Floor of Your Effectiveness Architecture

So, as you think about whether your strength is people, give yourself a bit of room for messiness! And here are some good observable hallmarks to look for:

1. You keep getting more direct reports added, or you're serially asked to manage people.

2. You're often called in to defuse emotionally fraught situations.

3. You're often asked to be a first point of contact for new stakeholders—new employees, new partners, visitors from outside the organization.

4. People seek you out as a mentor or coach.

5. You're inserted into moments when teams have to come together across silos, either in a leadership or a facilitation role.

People: What Am I Grappling with Today?

To start to understand how you work with people, we're going to assemble your "people mosaic." What kinds of human interactions make up your day? We'll look at three dimensions—the number of people in your interactions, the power dynamics in your interactions, and the emotions in your interactions.

People: The Numbers Game

There's a popular thought experiment that asks whether you'd rather fight one giant duck or 37 tiny ducks. It's a trick question. You shouldn't be fighting ducks: they're mean, and wildlife statutes prohibit it anyway. The underlying question is interesting though: Is your preference to deal with one big complex problem, or an array of smaller ones all at the same time? It's analogous to numbers of people in a meeting or other interaction, in a way. Some people prefer the intimacy of a 1:1; others like the grab-bag of more superficial interactions that happen in a larger meeting. With the caveat that, as per tons of research, meetings of less than eight people or so are more effective,[7] you have to, to some extent, "dance with the interaction size that brung ya." Our days at work don't always contain a ton of choice about the volume of people we're interacting with at any one time. To capture what your people interactions look like from a numbers perspective, break the 100% of a sample week into the following buckets:

   a. Truly alone doing work.

   b. One-on-one interaction.

   c. Small groups: three or four people.

   d. "Pizza box teams": 5–10 folks.

   e. Big teams: 11–50 folks.

   f. Crowds: 51 or more people.

People: The Power Game

Imagine your day consists of a single 1:1 meeting. Easy peasy, right? But wait: it's with your CEO. Or your most important customer. Feel your blood pressure rising? That's power dynamics in action. Our people interactions are inflected not just by how many folks are in them, but by the relative power positions of those folks. People both inside and outside your organization have power over you, and in many roles there are people you have power over as well. It sounds very stark to state it that way, but it's not a value judgment—just something that definitely does impact your people interactions. So, let's put together a quick map of the power dynamics in your

The Second Floor of Your Effectiveness Architecture

day-to-day work life. Similar to before, take 100% of an average week, and allocate it across the following buckets:

g. People who have more power than you, and work at your organization.

h. People who have the same amount of power as you, and work at your organization.

i. People who have less power than you, and work at your organization.

j. Customers, clients, and other people you are selling to or responsible for delivering things to, who work outside your organization.

k. Other people you might be responsible to outside your organization (government inspectors might be one example).

l. Vendors and other people who are selling to you, or responsible for delivering things to you, who work outside your organization.

People: The Emotion Game

Let's complicate the picture one more time. You've thought about how many folks you're interacting with at a time, and what the power dynamics are . . . now let's talk about emotion. How emotionally charged are the conversations you're in? And what are the emotions? Now, there are a million emotional taxonomies out there, often with dozens or even more than 100 emotions included. We're going to use a very simple one developed by the good folks at Disney for the movie *Inside Out*: Joy, Fear, Sadness, Anger, and Disgust—add two more emotions that they added in *Inside Out 2*: Anxiety and Embarrassment—and then finally add a base category,

Effective

Calm/neutral. Look at the times during the week you're interacting with people (basically anytime you're not alone, in person or virtually), and assign a percentage totaling up to 100% to how you feel during that time:

m. Calm/neutral

n. Joy

o. Fear

p. Sadness

q. Anger

r. Disgust

s. Anxiety

t. Embarrassment

You've got your "people mosaic" now: a multifaceted picture of how all your human interactions come together to form a typical week at work. Here are a few actions you can take immediately using this information:

1. *Look for the overall themes of each individual bucket.* When you look for the "big rocks" in each category, what jumps out to you? Do you spend much of your time in meetings with lots of people, or in 1:1s? Is most of your time spent with people inside or outside your organization? Do you spend a lot of time with your boss, or with people that report to you? And how do you feel during all of that? Are you mostly joyful or gagging with disgust? The nature of your people interactions matters—tapping different skills, and, as we'll discuss shortly, creating or destroying energy for you.

The Second Floor of Your Effectiveness Architecture

2. *Look for how the three buckets might be interacting with each other.* Now that you've got the big themes for each bucket (number of people in an interaction, power dynamics, and associated emotions), take a look at how they might relate to each other. Are you anxiously navigating large meetings of people senior to you? Are you fearfully handling 1:1s with customers? Calmly talking to small groups of vendors? What is your "average experience" or experiences? Can you start to make some generalizations about how the size of the group and the power dynamics are making you feel?

3. *Figure out your greatest energy source and what's depleting you the most. Then strategize.* Now that you've painted a basic picture of your people interactions, look at it through the lens of what amps you up and what drains you. This doesn't have to exactly correlate with the emotions: for instance, some folks are able to interact with angry customers all day long and actually derive energy from that experience. Others might be drained from the same thing. If you had to pick one category of interaction that really energizes you—and one that really saps your energy—what would you pick from the "people mosaic"?

People: What Does Disruption Look Like?

Conventional wisdom has it—and I generally agree—that people skills are the *hardest* to disrupt. As technology advances, and takes more and more procedural/mechanical work over, more and more human work will be about leveraging human skills to interact with human beings.

Consider the example of a highly automated resort hotel, in the near future. People check in on touchscreens and a keycard is automatically programmed for them. Once checked in, they head to the pool, where they swipe a bracelet to get towels from a locker and have

Effective

a pool chair automatically assigned. Then they order pina coladas via touchscreen as well and a robot rolls over with those too. Once they're done at the pool, they head up to their room and order room service off another touchscreen or on their phones via QR code. Room service is prepared by robotic chefs and delivered by robots as well.

Where's the human work in all of this? There's still plenty, it turns out. The four-year-old stung by a jellyfish at the beach still wants to be treated by a human medic. The only way to make the concierge superior to LLMs and web searching is to employ a human who's very familiar with the local area. Diners at the Michelin-starred hotel restaurant, unlike room service customers, want to talk to a human waitperson and sommelier about their order. When a robot's battery runs out mid hallway, delaying a critical kids-menu-hotdog delivery, a human manager has to be sent to make amends. (I'm using that specific example because the one item absolutely guaranteed to be edible on any hotel menu is the kids' hot dog. This I hold to be ironclad truth.)

All the human work I just described requires being good with people—both customers and co-workers. Especially assuming a world in which all hotels go more automated, these skills are not just desirable but an actual source of differentiation for organizations. Hence the argument for people skills being hard to disrupt: you might be doing a different job with them, but the skills themselves will keep you employed.

Nothing is completely resistant to disruption though—so here are a few provocations for ways that being strong in dealing with people may get disrupted:

- *People skills have to evolve when technology intermediates human interactions.* Know anyone who's lovely in person but awful over email? Charming on the phone but wooden on Zoom? A funny and engaging text-er but mysteriously miserable on Slack? The same underlying people skill is required—clear

The Second Floor of Your Effectiveness Architecture

two-way communication—but electronic intermediation asks you to up your game in medium-specific ways.

- *Context changes can demand different people skills.* Saying that the world moves faster today is a terrible cliché, but also one you can't ignore. This doesn't change the people skills you need, but it gives you a harder context to execute them in. It's easier, for example, to influence folks given more runway to talk to them. If you only have elevator-pitch timing, you'd better be pretty influential in 30 seconds! Moving across cultures and organizations also changes what good looks like and may disrupt your feeling of strength in people skills. Working in New York, I am sometimes told I'm excessively nice; when I did a multi-year stint in London, I was told I was brusque and rude. Same Melissa, two different cultural contexts with different behavioral expectations. (And yes—possibly an illustration of "there's no right way to be a woman in the working world"—sigh!)

- *Simple progress through your own career often disrupts the people skills you need.* Think about some of the categories of interactions you just catalogued—how many people you're interacting with, what the associated emotions are, what the power dynamics are. Now imagine you're the CEO of your company: all of that could change a lot, right? You might be speaking to massive town halls or doing more 1:1s with key leaders. You might be in highly emotionally charged dialogues or people might go to great lengths to mute their emotions around you. You might be the powerful person in every interaction or suddenly start interacting with government figures or other CEOs who are far more powerful than you. If your people skills remain exactly the same, you may face meaningful challenges—and the part of your skill set that'll be called upon the most is the versatility/curiosity/openness bucket.

Effective

So, if your strength is People—don't rest on your laurels. Remain alert to the nuances!

Technology: The Accelerant

I often ask people a question that stops them dead in their tracks.

"What does it mean to be good with technology?"

The notion of being good with technology is weirdly elusive. Some people define it on the basis of having memorized facts or learned methods (like programming languages); some define it as pure resourcefulness (the willingness to tinker until you get it right); some define it in fully mystical terms, like being a horse whisperer, but for bits and bytes instead of living creatures.

The reality is, working well with technology involves a strange mixture of optimism and pessimism. For any given piece of technology, you have to be curious and playful with it to really learn how to use it to its fullest extent, but you also have to understand its limitations to not over-rotate on what it can do. And then the same is true for all the technologies you use together.

Considering all of the above—and then adding in the unbelievable variety of technology and the fast rate of change—is it even possible to get to a list of what might make you good with technology? I would argue it is:

- *Curiosity about technology and willingness to experiment.* In *Surely You're Joking, Mr Feynman*, Nobel-Prize-winning physicist Richard Feynman captures this perfectly, with tongue firmly in cheek: "The trouble with computers is you *play* with them. They are so wonderful. They have these switches—if it's an even number you do this, if it's an odd number you do that— you can do more and more elaborate things if you are clever

The Second Floor of Your Effectiveness Architecture

enough, on one machine."[8] Whether you're a veteran of the Manhattan Project (like Feynman) or a crow (as we talked about previously), having an affinity for playing with technology serves you well.

- *Ability to de-bug.* In an ideal world, we wouldn't need to fix broken technology. But the reality is, even the best technology breaks down sometimes—and having the problem-solving skills to fix it, often through systematic trial and error, is thus a critically important technology skill.

- *Ability to interact with technology as a continuous extension of human work.* Dimitris Bountolos, Chief Information and Innovation Officer at Ferrovial (the global infrastructure company that, among other things, is rebuilding JFK airport), puts a premium on "citizen literacy: making seamless and fluid the incorporation of that technology in your daily routine."

- *Optimism/realism balance.* We all know Luddite curmudgeons (of all ages!) who just won't engage with technology. This is an unhelpful attitude. But equally unhelpful, I would argue, are the folks who just run around screaming about the AMAZING CRAZY IMPACT of every new technology that comes down the pike. THIS IS THE DAWN OF A NEW ERA, EVERYTHING IS GOING TO CHANGE, AND YOU ARE GOING TO GET LEFT BEHIND! It's exhausting, often associated with fearmongering to get you to BUY MY INCREDIBLE STUFF, and completely disingenuous. A sensible attitude toward technology—an *effective* attitude toward technology—balances excitement for new developments with tempered realism about what's actually taking place.

- *Understanding how different kinds of technology work together.* Getting how technology works with other technology can be

Effective

life-changing (or, at least, work-life-changing!) but we often get hampered by idealistic views of how this plays out in the real world. If you've ever uttered the phrase "What do you mean, those systems don't talk to each other?" then you know what I'm talking about. How you think technology integrates is not always how it does actually integrate. Tom Peck, CIO of food distribution company Sysco—and a former MIT CIO Symposium award winner—in fact cites orchestration among technologies and their providers as the really critical technology skill of the future: "[in my role I'm] getting people with different instruments, if you will, to play music together and do it brilliantly." To follow Peck's metaphor, it's not getting a single technology to play a great solo—it's conducting a symphony that sounds amazing when the whole orchestra plays together.

Technology: How Do I Know If This Is My Area of Strength?

Here are some observable hallmarks of being good with technology:

- You feel like technology support for the world. Everyone calls you for technology glitches.

- You fix many small technology issues on your own without calling the helpdesk.

- You often get enlisted as a technology trainer.

- You don't seem to spend a lot of time fighting with the various systems you use at work.

- You're often the one suggesting a more technologically-enabled way to solve a business problem.

The Second Floor of Your Effectiveness Architecture

Technology: What Am I Grappling with Today?

Moreover, each technology type has its own challenges. Similar to how we analyzed your people interactions, let's look at how you spend an average week with technology.

First, take 100% of your time and allocate it across these technology types:

- Technology where you *create*—this could be anything from Microsoft Word to advanced architectural modeling software. If you use the technology to make things, put it here.

- Technology where you *collaborate or communicate*—chat, email, videoconferencing, but also workflow tools like Asana go in this bucket.

- Technology where you *store, retrieve, and analyze information/ data*. Many functional systems fall into this category: systems that store and analyze finance data, HR data, supply chain data, and so on. Also in this bucket: technology like cash registers and flight-tracking software that sit squarely in the real world and allow you to capture/handle data from live events. Technology in this category doesn't have to be fully behind the scenes.

- Technology involved in *physical operations*. "Physical world" tools go here: stoves, front-end loaders, sailboat rudders. Fun fact: there is no human-created technology that can sniff out certain things as well as a dog's nose.[9] So, if you're the person that handles the airport beagle checking for heroin or rogue pineapples, you can classify your canine co-worker under "physical operations technology."

- *No technology at all*. This is pretty much just in-person conversation with humans. Everything else involves technology in some way, shape, or form!

This gives you a map of what your technological world looks like at work. Here are a few things that you can do with it immediately:

1. *Map out the technology areas where you are spending most of your time (and think about whether that's changing).* What kind of technology do you interact with the most? Are you spending all day in group chats? Entering data into systems? Swinging a physical axe? Creating endless PowerPoint slides? Has this changed recently, or does it seem poised to change? For instance, might better analytics systems mean you spend less time plunking data in, and more time chatting with co-workers about what that data means?

2. *Map out the technology areas where you feel most proficient.* Simply put: What kind of technology do you feel good at, and what kind bedevils you? Do you struggle with email? Do you feel particularly adept wielding a dog grooming brush? Are there nuances within categories? Do you feel wonderful writing in word processing technology and terrible creating presentations, or vice versa?

3. *Map out the technology areas that give you energy, and those that drain you.* This is a different question than what technology you feel good at: this is what technology you *like to use.* Where are you having fun? For example, I myself have gotten decent at using chat technologies over the years. And sometimes I genuinely enjoy it: it was an energizing way to communicate with 85 or so folks on my Capgemini Workforce & Organization team, for instance. We had a blast. That said, in entrepreneurial life I am on zero chat technologies . . . and goodness it's lovely. On the whole, it ensues that I find the medium tiring. What technologies do you feel that way about?

The Second Floor of Your Effectiveness Architecture

Technology: What Does Disruption Look Like?

As the future rapidly arrives, it seems like a no-brainer that folks who are great in the Technology area would be set up for success. But similar to Methods: yes and no. Technology, after all, evolves through cycles of being harder and easier to use. At times when technology is a bit more gnarly to deal with, folks with a strong Technology orientation excel. I have fond memories of my Dad getting us a Betamax VCR early in the 1980s. We were ahead of all the neighbors! We acquired a videotape of *The Wizard of Oz* and I watched it dozens of times. But then VCR technology took off—and everyone got this other format . . . VHS? And so on through DVRs and streaming. Heck, I still miss Tivo! The point here is not to discourage anyone from being an early adopter. Rather, it's to illustrate that the technology cycle turns fast and one's personal advantage erodes quickly as the underlying technology gets more user-friendly and open to a greater array of folks. For instance, if your job today is to code, you're at risk of both automation via AI as well as "vibe coding" tools. It's useful to have the underlying skills that make you great at the Technology area, like curiosity, playfulness, and a good scientific/technical baseline, but don't hitch your fortune to a particular technology.

Putting It All Together to Be Effective

I believe in strengths-based management—so it would be disingenuous to start ranting about how you need to fix your areas of challenge.

But there is something interesting in thinking through how you might be unintentionally stereotyped based on your combination of strengths and challenges, *with the goal of battling those stereotypes head-on*. Let's look at each combination of strengths and challenges and think about how people might perceive you.

If your strength is **Knowledge**:

- . . . and if your least strong area is **People**, you risk being perceived as unengaging and dry. You may not get full credit for what you understand because people find you inaccessible.

- . . . and if your least strong area is **Methods**, you risk being perceived as "book smart not street smart"—lacking an understanding of how the world works day to day.

- . . . and if your least strong area is **Technology**, you risk being seen as old-fashioned (no matter what age you are) and a bit egocentric—prioritizing your own brain over technology tools that could be helpful.

If your strength is **Methods**:

- . . . and if your least strong area is **Knowledge**, you risk being seen as a "corporate drone"—good at getting things done without truly understanding the things.

- . . . and if your least strong area is **Technology**, you risk being seen as slipping behind—great at older methods of getting things done but not up with the times.

- . . . and if your least strong area is **People**, you risk being seen as a cold-blooded operator—achieving results sometimes at the expense of the folks around you.

If your strength is **People**:

- . . . and if your least strong area is **Knowledge**, you risk being seen as an empty schmoozer—perfectly personable but content-free.

The Second Floor of Your Effectiveness Architecture

- • . . . and if your least strong area is **Methods**, you risk being seen as pleasant but chaotic—a lovely person who doesn't quite have it together.

- • . . . and if your least strong area is **Technology**, you risk being seen as all warm fuzzies and no practical effectiveness.

If your strength is **Technology**:

- • . . . and if your least strong area is **Knowledge**, you risk being seen as a pure geek who's disengaged with the underlying business.

- • . . . and if your least strong area is **Methods**, you risk being seen as using technology razzle dazzle to cover for a lack of systemic understanding.

- • . . . and if your least strong area is **People**, you risk being seen as robotic, embracing technology because you can't engage well with humans.

Thinking about your strongest and least strong areas—and leaning into your strength while being cognizant of how you might be perceived based on where you find more challenge—gives you real power.

As Chapter 4 Draws to a Close . . .

For everyone

- • Reflect on each of the Effectiveness Architecture "landscapes" (Knowledge, Methods, People, Technology). You've done a lot to create "an accounting" of what your world of work— and your own abilities—look like against those categories.

Effective

What questions are you starting to ask yourself? What has surprised you?

- Reflect on your area of strength and how it might get disrupted (or is being disrupted already). How are you future-proofing yourself?

If you're the boss

- Reflect on what your team's landscapes might look like vs. the Effectiveness Architecture—and critically, how they might look similar to yours or quite different. Does your team have very different human interactions all day than you do? Do they use different technologies than you do, or similar ones? Do you all have similar knowledge bases or very diverse ones? And critically: What do people's methods for putting it all together look like? Are they systematizing their work in ways different from each other or different from you? Or do you all take quite similar approaches?

If you're the big boss

- Reflect on your organization's Effectiveness Architecture—particularly what might need to change *other* than the skills of your population. It's a cliché, especially recently, that you need more folks with the Technology area of capability. As a funny former co-worker of mine used to say, "Do these folks grow on the digital talent tree?" It's worth thinking about whether that's actually the case, or whether you have folks with the right abilities to handle technology . . . but either the wrong actual technology in place or the wrong structures and processes around it. Similarly, many organizations bemoan

The Second Floor of Your Effectiveness Architecture

deficits around People capability, without considering issues like job design, incentives structures, or decision rights that may be inhibiting people's ability to work smoothly together.

We've thought a lot about what it means to be good at your job. So, let's now look at some jobs where you can't *not* be good. Where failure is not an option.

Chapter 5

The Shockingly Consistent Playbook for Effectiveness in High-Stakes Jobs

Imagine this: you've just done a 15-foot cannonball jump into the Hudson River. You've swum out 40 feet through choppy waters.

And the guy you did all this for? He doesn't want to be rescued.

This was a challenging day at work for New York City (NYC) firefighter Roland "Ro" Rodriguez. And honestly—a day at work that many of us couldn't imagine.

The question of how people do seemingly impossible jobs has plagued me for a long time. Both of my parents practiced medicine—a pretty high-stakes endeavor. And interestingly, one of the first career epiphanies I ever had—when I was still in elementary school—was that I *didn't* want a job where lives were on the line.

That idea scared me. How do people do it? How do they carry that burden?

Fast forward a few decades. I'm a long-time knowledge worker. As a consulting leader, I'm accountable to both my clients and my teams, but certainly no one's life is at stake. I'm in a weird state of the world—teamed up with brilliant folks and doing work we're all proud of . . . but also looking around periodically and going, geez, could the business of consulting, across very different companies, run a bit better? We just bungled *another* meeting; someone failed to have a tough conversation for the millionth time; no one seems to own any decision; every day is a bit of a goat rodeo.

We keep reassuring ourselves though: "We're not curing cancer." "We're not doing heart surgery." "We're not saving lives here."

So many times at work, we tell ourselves that what we're doing isn't *that* critical. Stop stressing; it's not that consequential. Don't take your job too seriously.

And don't get me wrong: that's TRUE. Only treating what's consequential as consequential is one of the most straightforward paths to a healthy workplace. I am in no way advocating for making every day feel like a dire struggle. Because it's not.

But there is an interesting question to be asked here. Many people do in fact have jobs where the outcomes are life and death. Do they have some wisdom for the rest of us sitting in apparently no-consequences-except-for-your-bonus land?

Yes. We do work differently when it really matters.

That's this chapter in a sentence. If you're pressed for time, you can stop reading right there!

I'm kidding. Please stick with me here—there's some really interesting learning to be had from people who do jobs that we've deemed un-screw-up-able. (Technical term!)

This chapter represents the amalgamation of that wisdom. I've interviewed some amazing folks who do high-stakes jobs, reviewed an array of research, and studied everything from job models to training manuals to understand how difficult, consequential work is codified. When we look at that body of insight against our Effectiveness Architecture, we find that high-stakes work is in fact set up very differently. There's an unwritten playbook for high-stakes work that is in many ways very, very different from how most of us go through our day to day.

Folks who do this work approach Knowledge, Methods, People, and Technology *quite differently* from the rest of us. There's a simplicity

Effective

and a clarity to their working life that helps them effectively take on the chaos of the world. And we could learn a lot from how they do it.

First, let's meet, and thank, the extraordinary humans who were kind enough to be interviewed for this chapter:

- Roland Rodriguez is an NYC firefighter.

- Anthony Tisdall is an air traffic controller for the Federal Aviation Administration (FAA) in Philadelphia, PA.

- Dr. Rebecca Parker is the Chief Coding Officer, TeamHealth and the Past President, American College of Emergency Physicians.

The Difficult Jobs Playbook: Knowledge

In air traffic control, it's all in the book. Specifically, the intriguingly titled *JO 7110.65 Air Traffic Control: FAA ATC/ATO Handbook* is the definitive account of what an air traffic controller should know to do their job effectively. Tisdall jokingly describes this epic tome as "about half my face thick." According to Amazon, it's 735 pages long and weighs 3.5 pounds, comparable to my neighbor's pet Maltese.[1]

Right now, you're probably having one of three reactions:

- If your job comes with extensive documentation like this, you're just nodding—this is normal.

- If your job doesn't, you might be thinking "Oh my goodness, if only my job came with an owner's manual."

- Or you're thinking "Thank goodness my job doesn't come with an owner's manual—I'd be so annoyed."

Earlier in my career, I was firmly in the "no owner's manual please and thank you" camp. If I wanted to be told how to do stuff,

The Shockingly Consistent Playbook for Effectiveness

I'd do something a bit less loosey-goosey than consulting. (Consultants, as I'm fond of saying, are cats, not dogs . . . don't try to teach us to sit!)

My views on the subject have evolved.

Based on my learning across large, complex client projects at large, complex organizations, and reinforced by my conversations with Rodriguez, Tisdall, and Dr. Parker, I've now come around to the view that there's a reason why we feel the need to spell out the knowledge needed for high-stakes work in such precise terms. When lives are on the line, the world is not loosey-goosey. As per the advertising campaign, there may be no wrong way to eat a Reese's,[2] but there are an array of ways you do *not* want people doing firefighting. Or air traffic control. Or emergency room medicine.

My personal worry was always that if someone told me exactly what I needed to know to do my job, I would turn into a mindless drone. What's interesting when you talk to folks in high-stakes jobs is that the opposite actually happens. Rodriguez describes how firefighters routinely sit around and scenario plan:

> *If we're not physically training, we're talking about it. We're having conversations about "Hey this is what we would do in this situation? Or say if I was struggling with that door to get inside that door with the tools that we have? Okay maybe is there a way we can position the tool in a certain way, or could we use two people instead of just one?" You're always looking for, is there some sort of like advantage we could use in X Y and Z situation?*

Because the group is aligned to the common notion of what he calls firefighting fundamentals—the basic stuff that doesn't change, everything from the flammability of materials to how humans breathe—they are able to then work on the stuff that *does* change all of the time.

A common knowledge base means they start the conversation well down the road, and can really solve new problems as they erupt. This is what Zeynep Ton, in *The Good Jobs Strategy*, refers to as a combination of standardization and empowerment.[3] Do things the same way every time, but give employees a voice in how they might be done better.

So, what does change? Rodriguez gave me a fabulous example. A key challenge in firefighting is breaking through doors. For various reasons, the people you're trying to save in an apartment may be incapacitated and not be able to open the door for you, so you're challenged to use various axes and other tools to get the door down and get in there, as quickly as possible. In one sense, this is Firefighting 101—the basic challenge of getting to the other side of a locked door was the same in 1725 as it is today. But as Rodriguez notes, you know what does change all the time? How we make doors and locks. A technician in Denmark develops a new mechanism for smoother deadbolts and 3 years later, an NYC firefighter is temporarily stumped as to how to jimmy it open. The basics of what you need to know are constant, but you have to keep testing and learning on the specifics.

Same situation in air traffic control: complete alignment on the basics plus a flexible body of knowledge equals work done right. Tisdall notes that while the Maltese-sized compendium of air traffic control knowledge is foundational to how he works, what makes him really effective on any given day is his detailed understanding of the airport where he works (Philadelphia):

> *The biggest knowledge as an air traffic controller is know-*
> *ing your facility and knowing the rules and regulations for*
> *your facility. I need to know every taxi way. I need to know*
> *the runways. I need to know the headings that we use.*
> *I need to know what's called missed approach procedures.*
> *If someone goes around, where are they going to go if you*
> *don't tell them something? These are the things that are*

The Shockingly Consistent Playbook for Effectiveness

really important because those are the things that become more important down the line if that unexpected thing happens.

In other words, while foundational knowledge gets him to work every day, it's local knowledge—learned on the job and ever-changing—that saves him when things get wild.

In Dr. Parker's case, the Knowledge part of the Effectiveness Architecture is also highly codified—but shockingly recently established. Emergency medicine as a discipline, incredibly, is only about 40 years old. As she explains:

*Emergency medicine was created after Vietnam. The vets and medical people came back and said, we were doing better evacuations, better MASH [Mobile Army Surgical Hospital] units, like the show M*A*S*H*, even as far back as the Korean War. This group said, we need to do this better at home.*

At the same time, there were a lot of advancements in trauma. There was a very famous trauma surgeon in Nebraska that was seeing patients die on the highway in the middle of Nebraska. And he said, we have to do this better. We have to have a trauma system. This led to the creation of trauma and EMS systems in the United States through congressional action and funding in the 1960s. And so all of these things culminated into a moment of the consideration of do we need a new specialty in this type of medicine, what is now emergency medicine, as well.

The birth of emergency medicine is in many ways the high-stakes version of the birth of The Knowledge for London taxi drivers that we learned about in Chapter 2. In both cases, folks got frustrated at something going wrong, be it lost passengers (low stakes) or people dying from avoidable causes (high stakes) . . . and as a result, they built a body of knowledge that bolstered a profession. The ailments being treated in emergency medicine are an amalgamation of every other specialty, but specifying a body of knowledge needed for the particulars of treating patients in an emergency context helps doctors save lives. Smushy general knowledge isn't enough. You need specifics—literally battlefield-tested specifics, in this case.

Back to the very premise of this chapter. Most of us don't work in jobs that have the Knowledge part of the Effective Architecture as well codified as firefighting, air traffic control, or emergency medicine do. But there are some concrete ways we can look at Knowledge differently, leveraging learning from high-stakes work. Here are a few thought questions to ask yourself:

- *What would a truly rigorous way of doing the things I do most often look like?* I'll illustrate this with an example from consultant-world: writing compelling presentation slides (or perhaps these days, editing a slide that AI generated for you!). I'd always been told that McKinsey consultants wrote presentations such that you could read each slide title in succession and understand the story. I cannot actually find an externally facing McKinsey document that says this, so it may be a consulting urban legend. More concretely, during my time at Deloitte we had very hard-and-fast actual rules about "what good looks like" in a presentation. Every fact had to be cited. Nothing could hit a level of complexity beyond, I believe, a fifth-grade level. At various points there were limitations on how small fonts could get. And so on. Slides were treated as a high-stakes enterprise—they were our way of communicating with the world. I've treasured and utilized that knowledge everywhere I've worked since—and none of

The Shockingly Consistent Playbook for Effectiveness

those subsequent companies have had the same rules about slideware. It's worth reflecting: What is your work's version of that? Are there things you could do more quickly, more accurately, and with greater impact and less risk, if your default was more rigorous and replicable? (Bonus points for teaching a more rigorous default to your team then . . . making everyone more effective.)

- *Is there rigorous knowledge I can "borrow" that would accelerate my effectiveness?* Vipin Gupta shared a wonderful example of this idea with me. When he joined Toyota Financial as CIO, he decided to take on some knowledge that on face, seemed afield of both financial services and building a healthy IT function:

When I joined Toyota I became a student of TPS or the Toyota production system. It's called a lean manufacturing system but it's really a behavior shaping system—a way for everyone in the organization, all the way to the lowest levels, to own the quality of what's produced.

Vipin's a-ha moment boiled down to the insight that working anywhere in the Toyota organization, not just on the factory floor, it made sense to know, and implement, "the Toyota way." He saw the task of building a game-changing IT function as behavioral, and he saw behavioral wisdom in TPS. This is highly analogous to how emergency medicine, as Dr. Parker describes it, has borrowed a number of techniques from the military—understanding that while the context might be different, there are common threads to the underlying challenges faced by each group . . . and the military had cycles and reps on getting things right that the brand new discipline of emergency medicine had not yet had.

The Difficult Jobs Playbook: Methods

When it comes to high-stakes work, Methods—clear, replicable ways of doing things—are front and center. Dr. Parker tells an amazing story of how deeply ingrained Methods around emergency response are. The morning of 9/11, a group of doctors were having breakfast at the community hospital nearest to ground zero. Their medical staff lounge oversaw the twin towers. When they saw, out their window, the first plane hitting the World Trade Center, without waiting for further information, they started taking action: "They knew immediately we're going to go upstairs, we're going to discharge everybody who's not a critical case, and we're going to cancel all the elective surgeries."

This was part of the hospital's formal disaster response plan, which the physicians knew because of prior planning and practice. The CEO and hospital administration set up a command center, as per disaster planning, while the emergency department staff started to receive victims. There was no question of what to do, they had a protocol and began to follow it at the earliest possible moment. Methods kicked right in.

Part of what makes the Methods part of the Effectiveness Architecture so potent in high-stakes work is, amidst what can sound incredibly random and chaotic, a high level of sameness day to day. The repetitive nature of high-stakes jobs is a feature, not a bug. As Tisdall explains, "80% of the time air traffic control is pretty routine. You're saying the same thing or doing the same thing over and over again." Dr. Parker notes that hospital emergency departments can generally project when patient admissions will surge within a 24-hour period—because on a data-driven basis, the flows are quite similar day to day. Repetition drives mastery—but also iterative improvement.

It's also fascinating—and telling—how much of the Methods side of high-stakes work is strictly proscribed. When Tisdall speaks about how air traffic controllers ward off mid-air or runway collisions, the very language he uses speaks to highly specified

The Shockingly Consistent Playbook for Effectiveness

methods for getting planes to not hit each other. He talks about "creating space" for planes—"separating" them. If two planes are too close, you work through a playbook of how to get them to be further apart—featuring well-honed procedures. Similarly, Rodriguez described certain kinds of rescues to me—burning-building rescues, water rescues, and so on—and in each case, despite a wide variety of ways the situation can play out, the basic steps are unchanging. The firefighter jumping into the water always has a rope around their waist; you always secure a firefighter rappelling into a burning building to the roof the same way, unless the roof is actually on fire (which is not as much fun as the song perhaps made it sound). The triage procedures in a disaster that Dr. Parker describes wouldn't work if the color-coding wasn't always the same simple four colors with the same meanings: red, treat immediately; yellow, treat soon; green, can wait; black, cannot be saved, offer supportive care.[4]

One thing that struck me in these conversations was that something people who study work are always pressing organizations for more of is effortlessly present in high-stakes work: role clarity. Complex, physically dangerous situations force the issue. You cannot simultaneously be the person rappelling down the side of the building *and* the person holding the rope. You can't be the air traffic controller watching the East runway *and* the air traffic controller watching the West runway. You can't be the doctor, the nurse, *and* the lab technician. Critical to the teaching of methods for high-stakes work is *making clear which role you're doing within the team.* And yet—in other kinds of work—we really muddle this one up! "This role is dual-hatted." "We've asked you to take on extra responsibilities." "You have a dotted reporting line." (Just triggered myself, typing that last one! It never ends well!) Or—we don't say anything at all and we assume folks within a team will just . . . figure it out. Which has a notably low rate of success.

Effective

All in all, the high level of Methods codification in high-stakes work has a lot to teach us. Here are a few thought questions to ask yourself to mimic how high-stakes work deploys Methods:

- *What's the routine part of my job? How can I make it more boring?* It sounds nutty to aspire to anything being more boring. Boredom's the worst! But consider how much of the reliability of high-stakes work relies on dull sameness; this routine march both hones skills to a fine point and allows mental space for when things get "interesting" (a five-alarm fire, a 10-car pile-up on the highway, two planes headed for the same airspace). Look at your calendar across a month—what's routine and what's not? Can you do things to make the routine more routine or systematized? Is it worth actually capturing in some way how you do the things you do most often? I'm not saying document every workflow or write a consulting-style playbook on everything (though I have absolutely seen folks give this advice), but it can be shocking how often you do certain things without a well-codified way of doing them. Get more boring on the boring stuff. The exciting stuff will thank you.

- *Do we know who's doing what? No, really, do we?* Especially as we become more senior in organizations, we often fall out of the habit of clarifying roles and accountabilities within a team. And then we wonder why things mysteriously are not getting done! As I noted in my article for *MIT Sloan Management Review*, this is going to feel odd when you start doing it: "This leadership move will feel strange. The first few times you step in to clarify who's responsible for which piece of what, it may feel ridiculously basic or didactic."[5] But looking at the level of continued role clarity in high-stakes jobs, there's such virtue in constant clarification.

The Shockingly Consistent Playbook for Effectiveness

The Difficult Jobs Playbook: People

If you've ever watched surgery, in real life or on the screen, you know what overcommunication looks like. "Scalpel?" "Scalpel." "Forceps?" "Forceps." Verbally confirming what instrument another medical professional is handing the surgeon is a critical safety procedure.

It turns out, air traffic controllers do this too. When Tisdall gives a pilot a critical instruction, procedure has him ask the pilot to repeat it back. If the pilot doesn't repeat it back completely or properly, they have to repeat it again—until they get it right. If he doesn't hear back exactly what he told the pilot, he has license to bug that individual until he hears his words coming out of their mouth. The importance of the communication drives a high level of precision.

Similarly, but in a very different context, Dr. Parker described to me a heartbreaking situation in which you absolutely must overcommunicate with simplicity and clarity: informing someone a loved one has died. Over the years, she has developed a well-honed way of delivering the most difficult news possible. She tells the story of the interventions that were tried, notes that she has bad news for the person she's speaking to, and then uses clear and precise language as to what happened. In order to avoid painful confusion, Dr. Parker notes: "you have to use words like 'dead'." In order to build her skills in conveying this message as clearly and compassionately as possible, earlier in her career she shadowed more experienced doctors in these conversations, to see how they spoke. Her communication is simple, precise, and clear—because it would be deeply unkind to screw it up.

Rodriguez, too, cites overcommunication as a necessary element of his job as a firefighter. The high levels of Methods clarity—and role clarity—that make firefighting possible have to be verbally reaffirmed to make sure everyone is aligned in the midst of danger and

Effective

chaos: "[You're constantly asking] What do we have? What are we doing? What are our roles for this situation?"

These steps may seem like the most basic level of communication, but they go wrong—wildly wrong—across many types of work that are not high-stakes. Think about the fundamental underlying principles implied in how Rodriguez, Tisdall, and Dr. Parker communicate:

- Establish agreement on the situation.

- Establish agreement on the course of action.

- Establish agreement on roles (as we just discussed for Methods!)

- Repeatedly confirm and reconfirm.

None of this is rocket science—but so often, when there's a debacle at work (or in life), it's because one or more of these steps has gone awry. In the corporate world we push away from communicating with clarity, often because we fear it. For instance, why say that dozens (or hundreds, or even thousands) of people are losing their jobs, when you could just say "It's a reduction in force?" And then we struggle to tell the exact truth in the moment when it matters. Jim Detert, a professor at UVA's Darden School of Business who specializes in courage, among other topics, cites telling the exact truth as one of the signature leadership skills of the current moment:

> *I think the ability to look people in the eye, and say I owe you the truth and even though I'm afraid of how this might go for all sorts of reasons, I am going to have this conversation—that can save us from threats to survival greater than we have ever seen in our lifetime.*

I don't know about you, but I'm pretty convinced!

The Shockingly Consistent Playbook for Effectiveness

So, let's look at some questions we can ask ourselves around the People portion of the Effectiveness Architecture—specifically, communicating more clearly—that will help us mimic the effectiveness of high-stakes work:

- *Where can I swap out particular words to make my statements clearer?* Think about Dr. Parker's guidance on communicating about the death of a loved one—you have to use the word "dead" because it's kinder to be clear. What's your work's equivalent of this? Where could you swap out a single word to be better understood, even if it feels a bit bracing? It can be hard to rewrite our whole scripts, but starting with single words and being consistent can truly shift the effectiveness of how you communicate.

- *Where do I need to ask for more clarification that I've been understood?* Workplace decorum may not allow us to use Tisdall's strategy with pilots—literally, repeat back to me every single word I just said—but in general, getting more clarification that you've been properly understood will also save everyone a lot of heartache. To make this strategy feel less onerous, you can build in rituals around reviewing next steps at the ends of meetings, a simple step that's often skipped in the hurry to get to the next 30-minute call. An even more subtle way of checking understanding might be to have someone prepare a follow-on communication to another audience, which you can then review.

- *If I need to build trust quickly, what is my approach?* In their respective interviews, Rodriguez, Tisdall, and Dr. Parker all highlighted the importance of building trust quickly as a core skill of their high-stakes jobs; this is a skill each has spent meaningful time honing. Whether you need someone to grab your hand to lift you out of choppy waves, to listen to you as you rewrite their

Effective

flight path in midair, or to give you lifesaving information about the gruesome injury you just incurred, getting a stranger to trust you is a critical ingredient in high-stakes work. We all have a version of this scenario, be it encountering new customers, onboarding new direct reports, or simply working with cross-functional team members for the first time. A fast-moving world means we need people to have faith in us pretty quickly. We will each have a different formula for doing so, appropriate to our personality, the person we're encountering, and the context of the encounter. That said, my interviewees did mention a consistent set of ingredients: appropriate demeanor (something we'll hear more about from UVA professor Jim Detert in Chapter 7); true up-front listening to learn the person's context; and simple phrasing on their side to be readily understood. These are not complex elements, but often all three go missing . . . and trust is lost at the moment you need it most.

The Difficult Jobs Playbook: Technology

High-stakes jobs have an intimate, interesting, and sometimes surprising relationship with technology. Here are three things that struck me in my conversations about technology with people who do high-stakes work:

- Sometimes old technology is chosen over new technology for reliability.

- People obsess about using technology properly.

- There's "technology for me" and "technology for others."

There are interesting implications for the rest of us in all these themes. Let's look at each of the three in turn.

The Shockingly Consistent Playbook for Effectiveness

Sometimes Old Technology Is Chosen Over New Technology for Reliability

Air traffic controllers call each other on landlines and track planes using a 1930s technology: radar. One of the latest and greatest technological developments in firefighting is a new type of rope. A lot of high-stakes work relies on really simple technology.

Why? There's a good and a bad reason. The bad reason is decades of underinvestment; to learn more about this in the air traffic control context, I recommend the excellent John Oliver episode on the subject.[6]

But the good reason is reliability. It's annoying when your smartphone call drops because you went through a tunnel; the same call drop is deadly if it happens for an air traffic controller who walked to the side of the tower with less reception. The same new thread that looks cool but frays quickly in your fast-fashion blouse is completely inappropriate for a rope that suspends a human being hundreds of feet in the air above a raging fire.

Old technology can be far easier to count on. So sometimes it's the surprising high-stakes choice.

People Obsess About Using Technology Properly

What struck me in my discussions with the folks who do high-stakes jobs is that, compared to what I've seen across client organizations and my own work alike, there was less emphasis on the technology itself and *more emphasis on getting every bit of use out of it*. Rodriguez, our NYC firefighter, explains:

> *[It's not enough to know the] specifications of the tools . . . what's important, is do you actually know how to use a tool effectively in four or five different kind of ways? It's challenging to really extract all the uses for a tool, to [know] how to manipulate the tool.*

It's fascinating to think about what it means to use a technological tool effectively in an era when we use so many dang technology tools. A Gartner study from 2023 noted that the number of apps the average office worker uses in a day is 11—nearly double the six apps/day they were using in 2019.[7] I can't help but wonder—yes, I'm saying that in a Carrie Bradshaw voice—can any one of us truly use nearly a dozen tools *well?* Or is one of the downsides of technological over-proliferation that we are all using many different technologies kind of poorly?

This sharp difference in how we use technology again showcases the effectiveness gap between highly consequential work and other work. Rodriguez does not have the option of being slightly clumsy with an axe (!); Tisdall can't get away with being anything less than crisp on how he reads a radar scan; Dr. Parker cannot explain to a patient's family member that their loved one died because someone couldn't quite get an IV in in time.

Me, on the other hand? This is my second book and I'm writing it in Microsoft Word, like I did my first book. Am I any good at using Microsoft Word? Oh goodness, absolutely not. I'm a non-Luddite who is not bad at testing/learning/debugging, and I would say I'm at maybe a 10% understanding of this critical piece of technology that's fueled, now, two really important efforts for me. I can barely align a paragraph and please—please—do not ask me to insert a graphic into a text in a way that might leave the text readable. And I've been on this dang program since the 1990s, when I was frantically hitting page count minimums using Courier New, double spaced, with some truly shady margins. (My friends-from-college group chat is having a hearty guffaw here.)

Now, you might say—and you'd be right—that technology is more and less central depending on what your job is. If you're the person controlling the robot arm holding an astronaut and keeping them from flying off into deep space, you should allocate more of your brainspace to technological acumen than Melissa the consultant, typing up her comical little *Office Space* references. Yes, so stipulated.

93

But isn't there something intriguing about the notion of a world where we use technologies at work more powerfully? Where each time we touch an app or tool, we do so with a sense of mastery? That's how technology operates in high-stakes work. And maybe it should work that way more broadly.

There's "Technology for Me" and "Technology for Others"

When I asked Dr. Parker about her experience of technology at work, she drew a distinction that I'd never heard before—but it was immediately, intuitively, illuminating.

> *My priority, and that of everyone around me, is the patient. So technology that makes sense for the patient really for me is important. Better cardiac stents, for instance, help people live longer, higher-quality lives. The difficult parts are the technology where the physician is the afterthought, like electronic medical records—those are often designed for the hospital and the insurance companies and not the bedside clinician.*

There's something really fascinating about what she's describing—a completely different level of engagement with technology that's truly aligned with her working priorities. How many times do we touch a technology at work that feels like it's not "for us"—like all its usefulness is designed for some other stakeholder? There's a constant low hum of irritation in using these technologies—a feeling of not-quite-rightness you can never shake. Conversely, when you use a technology that really helps you fulfill your priorities better, a positive emotional switch flips. It's exciting and fun, even when it's confusing and challenging. Conventional change management strategies will try to convince folks that there's a "what's in it for me" in every piece of

Effective

new technology . . . but at this point in history, I believe we all at some rock-bottom level grasp what Dr. Parker's describing. You know whether the technology is for you or not. It makes a huge difference.

Mindset Shifts: What It Means to Work Like It Matters

When work really matters, we do it differently in lots of interesting ways. But to close off this chapter, let's hone in on the key ways you can shift your mindset across your Effectiveness Architecture—changing how you think about Knowledge, Methods, People, and Technology—to work more like someone in a high-stakes job.

Table 4.1 lists the mindset shifts we've looked at.

Table 4.1 Mindset Shifts

	Many of us	Folks who do high-stakes work
Knowledge	Loose agreement on core knowledge across a given body of work; anxiety about experimentation	Tightly agreed core of knowledge plus a flexible, evolving set of specifics refined through testing and learning
Methods	High level of variation; often unclear roles	Highly replicable methods specific to oft-repeated tasks; roles are very crisply defined
People	Communication can be sparse and misunderstandings abound	Constant, almost repetitious overcommunication

(continued)

The Shockingly Consistent Playbook for Effectiveness

(continued)

	Many of us	Folks who do high-stakes work
Technology	Vary between being casual and focused users of our workplace technology	Get maximal use out of every technology, through a mixture of training and constant on-the-job retraining; really focus on "technology for me" and get amazing at it

As Chapter 5 Comes to a Close . . .

As we close out Chapter 5, let's talk about how you can operationalize each mindset shift—taking on the most helpful lessons of high-stakes work—depending on your role within the organization.

For everyone

- Knowledge: Nominate a "sparring partner" to work on the evolving parts of your knowledge base with (anything from leadership skills to new technologies).

- Methods: Figure out in what part of your work you're going to get more rigorous and boring.

- People: Choose a "word swap"—exchanging an ambiguous word in an important context for a clearer one—and stick with it for 6 months.

- Technology: Choose one piece of "technology for me" and get really, really good at it.

Effective

If you're the boss

- Knowledge: Consciously bring your team together, periodically, to talk about what they know. What is the common, perennial body of knowledge, and what's changing fast? How will you work on that evolution as a group?

- Methods: Look for places where the team can get "more boring." It may be helpful to take a step back and look for pieces of workflow that you may not think happen often . . . but do. You don't have to automate something with technology to make it more automatic; that said, making it more automatic will be incredibly helpful when the right technology does emerge to automate pieces.

- People: Talk to your team about where communication often slips—and develop some techniques for making sure everyone understands each other.

- Technology: Have an honest conversation with the team about what technology they feel is "for them," and what technology is honestly "for others." Then strategize about digging in on the technology "for them," and sensibly handling technology that realistically serves other stakeholders.

If you're the big boss

- Knowledge: Real talk about the age of AI. This is the moment to crisply define the core Knowledge of your organization. What is it that your organization knows, in its bones, that provides sustainable competitive advantage, and where must your organization's knowledge constantly evolve? This is particularly critical if you are *not* a Knowledge-centric organization; you don't want to be caught rudderless in a maelstrom of "you don't need to know anything anymore" hype.

The Shockingly Consistent Playbook for Effectiveness

- Methods: Similar to the question at team level, where can your organization get more boring, replicable, and rigorous? Organizations often have this down pat at "boulder" level, with well-honed Methods around common events like acquisitions or layoffs. But at "really big rock" level—things like confronting a new competitor or a major regulatory change—work is still often lumpy and unpredictable. More boring Methods can equal greater stability as the world continues to be rocky.

- People: Take a searching look at how your organization communicates with each other, starting with the simple lens of making yourselves understood. Put higher-order communications goals like inspiring and showing empathy to the side for just a moment, and look at *whether people are clear*.

- Technology: Work with your CIO (or yourself, if you are the CIO) to understand in broad strokes "what technology is *truly* for whom." If you looked honestly, who are the audiences for all your technological choices . . . and how is that impacting how others use that technology?

As this chapter wraps up, we're coming to a big turning point in the book.

You've learned a lot—and hopefully *thought* a lot—about what makes you, your team, and your organization effective.

So now we're going to flip the script, and talk about four trends (work intensification, emotional workplaces, hyper-transparency at work, and chaos) that challenge your effectiveness. The world of work is a bit wild at the moment—but the good news is, there are practical ways to make it more manageable.

Get ready to talk about work intensification—the effectiveness challenge you didn't know you were fighting.

Effective

Part II

Combatting Forces That Challenge Effectiveness

Chapter 6

Effectiveness Through Battling Work Intensification

I found a funny screenshot on my phone the other day. It was a little slice of my Outlook calendar from a prior job—I'd captured it because I'd hit a new peak, or a new low, depending on how you look at it: I was quintuple-scheduled.

That's not a typo. There were five concurrently scheduled meetings that I was expected to be in. Now, I could tell you that this was a consequence of my incredible effectiveness as a consulting leader—that I'd created unprecedented demand for my amazing skills. But instead I'm going to, as my daughter and her friends would say, "be so for real here": this is a normal thing that happens across the corporate world all of the time. We live in a world of so many meetings that it's not unusual for the same person to have four or five, or more, meetings at the same time. I knew one guy who'd figured out how to actually join multiple meetings at once, but even he, a certified legend, could only swing three at a time through a combination of phones and laptops.

The overgrowth of meetings is just one manifestation of a world of work intensification—the challenging phenomenon we'll spend this chapter talking about. Every kind of work has a version of this increasingly overloaded way of working; a 2019 *New York Times* article on the overloaded and chaotic days of app delivery drivers is stressful to even read, describing drivers trying to respond to an unpredictable series of app-driven "pings," all missing critical information, with too little time to do so, even as they physically dodge New York City traffic.[1]

As we'll talk about later in the chapter, this is a bit of a cyclical phenomenon: work gets more and less intense as social conditions and technology change.

Right now, though? It's a doozy. Work is highly intensified and that's a major challenge to your effectiveness. Let's explore how to battle this beast.

So, What Exactly *Is* Work Intensification?

I came across the specifics of work intensification when I was doing research for my first book, *Work Here Now: Think Like a Human and Build a Powerhouse Workplace*. Coming out of the COVID period, I was in a personal funk. Work seemed egregiously overstuffed. I started puttering around in Google Scholar for answers. Had the academic world figured out why everything had gotten so crazy? Hey, Siri, can you explain to me why work sucks?

I eventually came across a piece of research that truly shaped my worldview—turning my vague feelings about work badness into concrete vectors of terrible. Apparently, for years, researchers had been studying this thing called work intensification, where working conditions become more challenging due to shifts in the underlying nature of the work itself. The explanation that really crystallized my understanding originally came from Eurofound's Sixth European Working Conditions Survey,[2] and was further clarified by the UK's Trade Union Congress some years later.[3]

This seminal research defines work intensification in three ways:

1. Too many tasks in too little time.

2. Work that is too interdependent.

3. Work that is too emotionally inflected.

In this chapter, we'll look at categories 1 and 2, and understand how best to combat them, leveraging our Effectiveness Architecture. Then we'll devote our whole next chapter, Chapter 7, to category 3—emotionally inflected work—recognizing that it's a special challenge all on its own.

Sheer Overload: Too Many Tasks in Too Little Time

To think about this category of work intensification, first imagine carrying a bag of sponges. It's a breeze! Now, imagine the sponges have been replaced by bricks of exactly the same size. Not so easy to carry that bag, is it?

The difference between sponges and bricks is density. That's what task overload does to work—each hour is denser with tasks (partly because they're due sooner). You may be working the same number of hours, more hours, or even slightly fewer hours—but you experience work as *heavier*. It takes more out of you, just like carrying those bricks. It's harder to do 14 back-to-back video calls in a day than four. It's harder to pick more strawberries or load more warehouse pallets in an hour. It's harder to see more patients in a day, teach more students in a class, or manage twice as many direct reports as you used to. It's the same amount of day, the same amount of you, but more is being asked of you.

Effectiveness Through Battling Work Intensification

To understand a bit more about what task overload looks like on the ground, let's go back to the research we referenced in Chapter 2—the April 2025 study in which my company, Anthrome Insight (with Patrick Hyland, PhD, and hosting analytics partner Remesh), surveyed 1,000 people regarding work intensification.

Were these folks suffering from task overload? Oh yes! When asked what was making them feel overwhelmed, 56% noted high workload/task volume and 32% said tight deadline/time constraints.[4] Reading the most upvoted qualitative comments (i.e., the comments from participants that resonated most with their fellow participants), you really feel the waves of pain:

- "Tight deadlines and a large amount of work."

- "Too many projects at one time."

- "Hectic deadlines and having to ensure that everyone I manage is up to date."

- "They just keep adding . . ."

Oof, that last one! That's what makes us feel a bit like Sisyphus from Greek mythology, rolling a rock uphill only to have it roll back down . . . they just keep adding.

In general, our research showed that task overload cut pretty equally across different groups. Industries experienced similar amounts, folks from different genders or ethnicities had pretty similar experiences, different functional groups (HR, IT, etc.) were not that different . . . this issue runs pretty rampant.[5]

Intriguingly, we also found that task overload went all the way up the ladder—and in fact the C-suite and senior leadership were 15% *more likely* than others to report a high volume of work, and 66% of their self-reported reasons for feeling overwhelmed related purely to tasks and time.[6]

Why is this going on? A few hypotheses are possible. Decades of cuts to administrative assistants may have caused tasks to land back on executives' plates.[7] A more complex and unpredictable world has actually sent work back up the corporate ladder—demanding more skills/experience. Or years of underinvestment in developing leaders at lower levels has left senior management with an underskilled layer below them, forcing them to address more themselves.

In any case, finding out that leaders at the very top of organizations are overloaded with tasks too shocked me. And in a strange way saddened me as well. If the folks in the C-suite are struggling with task overload: (1) what hope is there for the rest of us and (2) importantly—what impact is this having on the rest of the organization?

Strikingly, our research also showed that the C-suite and senior leadership are almost 2.5 times more likely to always feel overwhelmed than the rest of the organization.[8] When that's the tone at the top, we may all be in trouble.

Death by Committee: The Challenge of Interdependence

"I feel like firing 14 chairmen of committees. I can't stand it anymore. I'm sorry. It's my fault. I'm the boss."

—*Jamie Dimon, leaked townhall transcript*[9]

Interdependence: a force so awful, even the CEO of a more than 300,000 employee company feels it acutely.

So, let's look at what interdependence is, and why it makes work worse.

Interdependence is in fact a fabulous example of good intentions gone terribly wrong. Remember when we talked about collaboration at the beginning of Chapter 4? All of that terrific working together

Effectiveness Through Battling Work Intensification

during the prehistoric hunt, signaling to each other using our unique evolutionary adaptation, the white sclera of our eyes?

Fast forward 5,000 or so years, and much like that time you ate the whole pint of Chunky Monkey, we're gone completely overboard on a basically good thing. Modern corporations are a tangled web of interlocking teams, interconnected initiatives, scrambled reporting lines, and fuzzy-at-best decision rights.

It's good, and it's right, for us to need each other—but when everyone needs everyone for everything else all the time, that's exhausting. People needing each other is a funny paradox, as one research report notes: "Team interdependence can reduce members' vulnerability to [negative emotional states] by facilitating a gain in support resources (i.e., social support). On the other hand, team interdependence may also increase members' vulnerability to [negative emotional states] via the depletion of regulatory resources manifesting in the form of emotional exhaustion." In other words, teaming up with people—operating interdependently—both builds us up and wears us down.[10]

In our work-intensification study from April 2025, respondents who needed to involve a large number of people to do their work were 49% more likely to feel always or often overwhelmed than their peers who only needed to involve a small number of people. Conversely, respondents who felt they were highly effective were 16% more likely to report being able to work largely independently.[11] Losing control of your work because so many people are involved is exhausting—particularly when, as in so many companies, you individually are held accountable for an end result it seems everyone has their decision-making hands on.

Think of interdependence like salt in cooking. You need it, and to a certain point it makes everything better. But put too much in . . . and the food is inedible.

On that basis, a lot of modern work at large, complex organizations has become hard to choke down.

Effective

Work Intensification: We've Been Here Before, Historically

Let me answer the question that inevitably comes up at this point: "Melissa, when you say *work intensification*, you're not just talking about hard work, are you?"

Nope. Absolutely not.

I would actually argue that work intensification is the enemy of truly focused hard work. In our late-20th/early-21st-century mania for optimization, we've crammed too many objects into the junk drawer of work, and now the drawer is overflowing . . . and mostly full of junk. The notion that we could optimize infinitely, without passing some sort of efficient frontier where things would start to get suboptimal again, was marketed very effectively by [hangs head] the consulting industry. Consider this question: When was the last time you heard someone define a *limit* of productivity, on an individual, team, or organizational basis? The assumption is infinity . . . and thinking about this for 2 seconds rationally, that *cannot* be true.

What's interesting is that we've lived through this before.

Pre-Industrial Revolution, agrarian work had natural limits. You didn't make some individual decision about when your working day was going to be over: the sun set. You didn't decide on a random sales blitz: it was pouring with rain outside, and you couldn't take your goods to market. You didn't strategize about the seasons, sneakily moving your Halloween candy orders into August: it got cold and the harvest ended. Were folks always trying to do things better and more efficiently? Of course! But were there places where you had to just *stop*? Yes.

But with the advent of the Industrial Revolution, and the introduction of more technology into work, all bets were off. Aided especially by advances like electric light, suddenly work started to spring out of its bonds. Researchers at the Massachusetts Institute

Effectiveness Through Battling Work Intensification

of Technology aggregated estimates of working hours across the centuries, and the differences are stunning. In the 13th and 14th century, folks worked in the 1,400–1,600 hour a year range; in the 19th century, they worked more than twice that—around 3,600 hours a year![12] What's fascinating is that these differences in hours don't even take into account the notion of work density. Industrial Revolution workers were grappling not just with more hours, but with more tasks in less time than their pre-Industrial Revolution counterparts. They would have been hugely grateful for a desk and some salad. Their working lives often stank and sometimes killed them.

This is where the relevant case study for work intensification comes in though: we eventually, in many ways, cleaned up industrial work in ways that has great relevance for knowledge work. Economist Robert Gordon has a great pithy description of how we got to the mid-20th-century productivity boom by, in part, finally getting good at leveraging technology, using cars as an example: "While the inventions came in the late 19th century, it took a lot of time to figure out how to use them productively . . . So it took a good 20 years for the first cars to come out, and trucks. And then another 30 years for them to make their way through the economy."[13] It wasn't enough to just be able to kind of, sort of, do stuff; we saw productivity gains when we really got human and machine working together in the right way.

That's something to aspire to.

How Work Intensification Challenges Our Effectiveness

Conventional wisdom—or rather, a rogue's gallery of hustle-culture snake-oil sales people—would tell us that work intensification is just a worker happiness problem. It's just annoying to have to actually do so

Effective

much work, right? Y'all are slackers who just want to laze about snuggling with your Doodles, running errands and . . . gasp . . . eating lunch. You want to take a moment and actually think or rest? You'll be overtaken by the army of hustle drones who can't stop, won't stop.

A more helpful and research-backed, but still incomplete, view is that work intensification is just a burnout issue. This is a humanistic take: we overloaded work and now people are right to be exhausted.

But here's the thing about work intensification: it whacks not just worker health and happiness, but *effectiveness*. Jamie Dimon isn't ticked off about 17 committees because he feels tired . . . he's upset because all of that mess clouds the path to profit.

More tasks and more interdependence get in the way of getting things done. Let's look at some simple ways work intensification challenges each aspect of the Effectiveness Architecture, and just for fun—in this chapter and the next few—we'll score how tough the challenge is on a scale of 1 to 10.

Work Intensification and Knowledge: Impact Level 5/10

Work intensification *obscures* Knowledge. Imagine you have to give a speech on something you know very, very well. Even if you don't love public speaking, this doesn't seem too rough, right?

Now imagine giving that speech under two different sets of conditions:

1. In one set of conditions, people are constantly yelling stuff unrelated to your speech as you speak. It's distracting, right? Even if you recognize much of it to be nonsense or not urgent, you can't help getting thrown off every time someone interrupts.

2. In the other set of conditions, people aren't yelling unrelated things—they're telling you how to give the speech, from many

Effectiveness Through Battling Work Intensification

different perspectives, and they're insisting on giving parts of it themselves. Again, you're finding it hard to express what you know!

Scenario 1 is task overload; scenario 2 is excess interdependence. And you can see how both states of the world meaningfully compromise your ability to manifest what you know.

(If that reference to being interrupted stressed you out—never fear! Later in the book we'll explore what Dr. Rebecca Parker, our sage emergency room physician from Chapter 5, recommends to combat interruptions . . .)

Work Intensification and Methods: Impact Level 8/10

Work intensification *swamps* Methods. This is something I hear over and over from executives all the way down to frontline workers: "I used to know how to get the important stuff done, but now I don't anymore." You can have the most beautiful system for getting work done effectively, and work intensification will, through a sheer excess of touchpoints, completely overwhelm it. Interdependence is a particular killer on this front—if everyone and no one owns everything, do anyone's Methods even really matter?

Work Intensification and People: Impact Level 9/10

Work intensification, at its worst, *can almost disable our ability* to handle people. Why? Let's come back to that burnout conversation. If you are personally burned out by intensified work, even if you have real strength in the People section of the Effectiveness Architecture, your emotional energy to deal with others is meaningfully depleted. It gets worse, though: because you're likely operating in an atmosphere of overall intensification, the other folks around you have similarly low emotional tanks . . . and you're all interacting with each other in a highly diminished way. Similar to Methods, at a certain point of work intensification you lose People skills as an effectiveness method altogether.

Work Intensification and Technology: Impact Level 4/10

Work intensification *impairs* our interaction with technology. Of the four categories of our Effectiveness Architecture, technology capability is least hard hit by work intensification. When we get besieged by tasks or mired down by interdependence, we may feel a bit maladroit, maybe operate a bit less curiously, and perhaps forget a password or two, but in general our ability to navigate technology is less compromised than other drivers of effectiveness.

Work Intensification: How We Fight Back

Work intensification can feel like a really insurmountable problem. There's a good, technical reason for this: like so many of what sociologists call "wicked" problems, it's ownerless. There's not one single person in the world, in your industry, or in your company causing it. I mean hey, if you could pin it down to just that person, you'd get them fired, right? (Who am I kidding . . . they'd probably get promoted instead. Excuse me while I bang my head against the keyboard for a moment.) Rather, work intensification is the culmination of a million bad working practices and unintentional consequences of technological progress.

So when we did our April 2025 study on work intensification—focusing on individual strategies to fight back—we did get some pushback from audiences. Fix the underlying work, they said, don't glorify muddling through it. Look, I don't disagree. The underlying work needs fixing and that theme was front and center in my first book, *Work Here Now*. But we can't wait for the cavalry to ride in,

Effectiveness Through Battling Work Intensification

even if that cavalry includes ourselves. While we work on the problem of intensified work, we have to, person by person, confront the issue of doing battle with it day to day—even if it feels impossible. So, let's see what Anthrome Insight's research turned up.

Our study found that *people who passionately combat all three aspects of work intensification feel dramatically more effective.* Some 1 in 8 respondents are what I called in an article for *MIT Sloan Management Review* "desert flowers"—able to thrive in difficult conditions.[14] This group strongly believes in, and acts on, reducing task load, reducing dependence on others' work, and reducing emotion in the workplace. This group is 119% more likely to feel highly effective than their peers who are less consistently committed to battling work intensification. They may not always feel great . . . they are almost four times more likely to always feel overwhelmed. But they are pushing through the momentum—they are, strikingly, almost four times as likely to see themselves as highly motivated.[15]

There's something special going on with this group's effectiveness amidst work intensification—and we can all learn from it.

First, and simplest, they are engaging with work itself as part of the problem. So often we are pushed to believe that "the work is the work"—conflating the natural difficulty of operating in a complex world (fair, valid) with unneeded complexity, overload, and time pressure that we ourselves introduce (not logical at all). It's helpful to remember that the message is not "accomplish less and slow down"— it's actually "do fewer things, get more done, and have more runway to speed up when you need to." I get the odd brickbat or two that I'm somehow advocating for ignoring shareholders' demands for profit, painting a slower path to return on investment, or just generally babying workers. This is a classic straw man—a passionate defense of the status quo that many folks benefit from *not* fixing. Once you say the goal is the goal but the work might not be quite right . . . you're off to the races.

112

Effective

Second, this group of "desert flowers" is willing to take actions that, as I note in my MIT article, may be seen as countercultural in some organizations: giving tasks away and working more independently.[16] Consider the classic stereotype of someone who's awesome at their job. They "put in 150%" and "they're an amazing collaborator." Translation: they take on an infinite number of tasks and work with everybody all the time. The desert flowers—the folks dealing with work intensification the best—do the opposite! They give away tasks that don't fit their mandate and they consciously do things to work more on their own. Let's face it, in many working cultures that sounds a bit weird, right?

Worried that your strategies to address the work deluge will make you a pariah? The following are a few angles you can take to reduce tasks and/or work more independently—fighting work intensification like a "desert flower."

Create a Natural Structure

Create a natural structure and mechanisms around delegating work as well as sharing it laterally. Think about it this way: there are three directions work can go: up, down, and across. If you can truly succeed at passing work back *up* the chain, you're a genius and I'd like to interview you for my next book (whatever that is on!). So that leaves us with two directions, down and across. There's a great array of literature on delegating properly, so I won't go into excess detail here, except to say: be incredibly conscious about what *keeps you from delegating work* and then *strategize to avoid whatever that is.*

For me, two things kept me from delegating work: working at a fast pace, and my own high standards. Once I realized this, I put mechanisms in place that addressed those issues head-on. For instance, I would introduce a conscious stop very, very early in a project, where—with plenty of time in the equation—even at a fast pace I'd have time to delegate, review work, and coach on outputs.

Effectiveness Through Battling Work Intensification

This also helped solve the high-standards issue: one can iterate to success given enough ramp time.

The more interesting question, though, is how to uncontroversially pass on tasks not to your junior folks, but to your peers. I'm not advocating for a game of "hot potato" with unappealing work—in most workplaces, sadly, that's going on already. Picture a swap meet instead. Especially in matrix organizations, it can be genuinely unclear where a particular task should fall; back to the theme of not assuming "the work is the work." Not every task may initially land with its natural owner. Having periodic connection points—like a designated section of a staff meeting—where folks can share what they're working on and evaluate if they're the exact right person to carry it forward—can truly help clarify this. Done right, it can put work back in the hands of the person truly positioned to be effective at it—and can also generate stretch and collaboration opportunities that many folks might value. There's a reason why swap meets are kind of fun.

Reduce Group Size

For more independent work, consciously work to reduce the group size of everything, all the time. In Chapter 9, we'll get into some German research around complexity that really illuminated the subject for me. (Made it simple, even!) Quick preview: one of their fundamental findings was that larger groups are more unwieldy—citing, frankly, centuries of work to this exact point.[17] This gives us an intriguing brute-force strategy as we try to work more independently, for our own sanity and effectiveness: *just get groups smaller*. Imagine two scenarios: a team of 19 people, and a team of four people. In the team of 19 people, it can get very sticky to ask for permission to just run off and work on something alone before bringing it back to the group. With a team of four people, in contrast, it's natural for all four team members to work independently then come back together—modeling the "figure 8" collaboration we should all be seeking.

You may comment here, quite sensibly: "But Melissa, I'm not in charge of the size of any of the teams that I'm on." Fair! At a couple of jobs, I and others have fought to no avail to have certain formal team sizes reduced to maximize effectiveness. The reality is, overly large teams are created out of fear—both fear of leaving some stakeholder group out and fear of any voice getting enough share of the dialogue to challenge the power of the team *above* the team. You're not going to wave a magic wand and make that fear go away. Big teams have the same effect on the leaders in charge of them as eating a giant plate of French fries: it's somehow calming, even if it's really not good for you.

What you can do—and what I suggest in my March 2025 MIT article on bolstering accountability, because this move both makes you more effective *and* others more accountable—is form some subteams or subcommittees.[18] Telling your boss you want to reduce the size of some middle-management leadership team is going to set off the blood pressure alarm on their smartwatch; statements like "can Devon and Mary Sue and I go figure this one question out?" are a lot better received. Then, within the subcommittee, you're well positioned to divide and conquer—giving you that space for independent work where so much effectiveness lives.

Drive a Prioritization Conversation

Feed a truly holistic picture back to the leadership level above you of everything going on—and drive a prioritization conversation. Back to that issue of work intensification being ownerless: sometimes you can start the process of de-intensifying work simply by flagging all

Effectiveness Through Battling Work Intensification

the things going on (and how interdependent they are). This conversation, of course, looks very different by level and context. A frontline retail manager might gently flag to regional leadership that corporate has asked them to do an inventory reorganization at the same moment as a long-planned seasonal switchover in merchandise; a CEO might assertively tell their board that certain minor technology initiatives have been placed on hold to create space for a bigger set of AI pilots.

What's critical here are a few things:

- Too many tasks are happening, often too interdependently, because different owners have generated them (with good intentions generally).

- Leaders at a higher level are genuinely not aware (often this is not a skills issue; just a function of crowded internal communication channels).

- You have a true vehicle to make these leaders aware of the organizational "traffic jam" in a thoughtful and measured way. (Screaming "LOOK AT ALL THE STUFFFFFF" will not work—trust me, I've tried.)

Done right, this sort of communication can truly help de-intensify work. For one organization I worked with, for instance, leaders made the folks they reported to aware of how many high-intensity processes and technology roll-outs were all happening during a dizzying year-end. No one had realized it was happening all at once, and as a result some timelines got pushed back, meaningfully lightening the load on folks during an already busy moment. Before anyone starts whining about return on investment, let me also assure you that each process was more productive due to the altered timelines; funny how nothing gets done when everything's due at once!

As Chapter 6 Comes to a Close . . .

So, as we bring this chapter to a close, let's talk about how we get started on the journey of being effective *despite* work intensification.

For everyone

- *Take a step back and understand where your work is intensified—clearly parsing out between "intense business need" and "this has gotten a bit silly."* Circling right back to where this chapter opened: hard work is not intensified work. If you're in the middle of a product launch or a natural disaster, you're not what this chapter is talking about. However, if you're trying to get an approval from 17 committees (Jamie, I see you!) or running through a 34-item to-do list . . . that is work intensification and you need to mentally call it out. It won't solve itself. And consciousness is the first step.

- *Identify a few strategies to combat work intensification (by reducing either tasks or interdependence).* Try them out one by one, giving each one a lot of space to work. Let me express this with great passion: do *not* combat work intensification by freaking out and trying a bunch of strategies at once, thus creating . . . more work intensification. Rather, grab a single strategy (e.g., forming some subcommittees, or doing a better job delegating to your team) and try it out. If it works, make it routine; if not, try something else. Work intensification is a strange beast: every workplace is unique; there's no set formula, just a nice array of strategies to try.

- *Develop a fabulous elevator pitch for what you're seeing to be effective at instead of engaging in intensified work.* Sadly, not everyone you encounter at work will have read this chapter! So folks who confuse "bulk or complexity of workflows" with

Effectiveness Through Battling Work Intensification

"actual effectiveness" may challenge your efforts to stem work intensification. Be ready: have an elevator pitch on how you plan to be more effective by de-intensifying work, complete with a "what's in it for [whatever stakeholder starts asking questions]." You can leverage the Effectiveness Architecture here, saying things like "Engaging in fewer cross-functional initiatives gives me the time I need to lean in on my team's development" (People) or "Shifting that meeting to next month is giving us time to test whether AI can take over some of the project" (Technology).

If you're the boss

- *Consciously examine the impact your own work intensification may have on your team.* If you're a leader, your work being intensified hits your team, too. Some of our data from the April 2025 study makes this quite apparent. Nearly three-quarters of the C-suite folks we surveyed (73%) cited excess work as a reason for feeling overwhelmed—and the impact of this was felt clearly by the layer of leadership below them, 29% of whom cited the C-suite's inability to prioritize as a driver of *their* feelings of overwhelm.[19] Overloaded executives overload other leaders, and the weight just passes on and on down the chain. Once you've taken a step back and looked at your levels of work intensification, take stock of how it impacts your team. Quite often, for instance, "working managers" overloaded with their own tasks don't spend enough time on people development.

- *Stop yourself from intensifying work.* Don't assign tasks of questionable value, don't put together overly large teams, and don't design overly complex processes. I know, I know, no one thinks they're assigning bogus work, or putting together teams and processes nonsensically. But we all get a bit unintentional,

Effective

and that's where the trouble starts. Put up some common-sense mental gates to help stop yourself from assigning excess tasks or creating excess interdependence. If a process cannot be simply described without an elaborate visual diagram, or if it involves a large number of people, it's too complex. If a task does not "earn its place" among other tasks—particularly if it will not have the same value to the task-doer that it has to you—think twice about assigning it. Don't create "bigger than two pizzas" teams (more than 10 people). These rules seem astonishingly simple, but it's shocking how often these basics go awry.

If you're the big boss

- *Ask folks at all levels where work is getting intensified . . . then do something about it.* I can take no credit for this strategy: prominent figures as diverse as Sundar Pichai and Bob Sutton/Huggy Rao have suggested it. In 2022, Pichai implored Googlers to participate in a "Simplicity Sprint"—helping identify where the noise of intensified work is getting in the way of the signal of effectiveness.[20] In other words: help debug the organization. Sutton and Rao advocate for the same throughout their terrific book *The Friction Project*—even noting that folks can be given a powerful identity as "friction fixers."[21] In both cases, the message is the same: your workforce knows where work has gotten messy, and they'll lead you to how to fix it. Ask where work is too much, and they'll tell you. But then you have to actually take action!

Good news: we've talked about two of the three ways work intensification causes us problems. Now on to Chapter 7, where we talk about the third vector of work intensification: overly emotional workplaces.

Effectiveness Through Battling Work Intensification

Chapter 7

Effectiveness Through Managing Workplace Emotion Appropriately

In space, some folks can actually hear you scream. At least, they can hear you scream at your fellow astronauts.

A 2023 NASA document called *NASA-STD-3001 Technical Brief: Behavioral Health Mishaps* makes for an interesting read on the interpersonal challenges of space travel. It's not all smooth sailing, hundreds of miles above planet earth: the document cites at least three missions (Soyuz 21, Salyut 5, and Soyuz TM-2-Mir) that were terminated early or even evacuated due to "interpersonal issues [or] conflict."[1]

A Harvard Medical School article quotes a cosmonaut's diary on one of these tense missions:

"Today was difficult," Lebedev wrote about crewmate Anatoly Berezovoy on their 60th day in space. "We don't understand what is going on with us. We silently walk by each other, feeling offended. We have to find some way to make things better."[2]

Who among us, at work, has not at some point silently walked by a co-worker feeling offended? The cosmonauts' struggles are very relatable.

That said, it may seem extraordinary to end a complex, expensive undertaking like a space journey because people are struggling to get along. But thinking back on our learning from Chapter 5, when the stakes are high, you cannot take the risk that bickering leads to someone's death. So, at least three times, a government has taken the extreme step of pulling the plug on a space mission where emotions ran too high.

Back down here at sea level or thereabouts, we don't have the option to call it a day because Bud from Accounting and Sally from IT don't see eye to eye on the timeline for the ERP implementation and keep duking it out on Zoom.

But emotional workplaces are a tremendous challenge, nonetheless. Gallup tracks negative emotions at work—measuring how many workers report feeling them "a lot of the day." The data, as reported in December 2024 (but consistent across the last 5 years), is bleak: 51% of folks were stressed, 40% were worried, 22% were sad, and 18% were angry.[3] That's alarming—particularly the finding that nearly one in five workers is angry. That cannot feel good for them or the people they interact with.

Anger definitely showed up in Anthrome Insight's April 2025 study. Fully 28% of our respondents reported dealing with angry co-workers, bosses, or customers, or some combination thereof. That group, in turn, was about 30% more likely to always or often feel overwhelmed than the rest of the population. When you dial in on the angry-customer phenomenon, the data gets really alarming. Fully half of our respondents in customer-service-specific roles reported often dealing with angry customers, and as a result, customer-service folks were a whopping 45% more likely to feel always or often overwhelmed than the overall population.[4]

There's a reason why excess emotion in the workplace is considered the third dimension of work intensification: the same work gets much harder to do when you're surrounded by negative emotions

Effective

(others', or your own). So, let's talk about how we got here—why workplaces are experiencing a high-drama moment—and then let's explore what we do about it.

The High-Drama Workplace: How We Got Here

There's no easy, simple answer that explains exactly why we're working steeped in so many negative emotions right now, or why workplaces are rife with conflict. Rather, we're seeing the intersection of a few factors.

Put all these factors together—a bunch of folks who may not interact regularly, often intermediated by technology, in a world that's talking and not listening and fighting with itself . . . and, of course, you have a recipe for emotional, conflict-laden workplaces.

The World Is Conflicted and Polarized—Far Beyond the World of Work

Researchers studying peace came to a disturbing conclusion recently: 2023 was the most violent year on record, globally, since 1946.[5] In the United States, political polarization has certainly surged; Gallup data suggests that about a fifth less people identify as "moderates" today than did so in 1992, meaning more people are at either end of the political spectrum than before.[6] Whatever your beliefs, there's no arguing that we're at odds with each other, and that this overall mood of clash is not helping us get along at work.

Technology Can Amplify Emotional Arousal, Frustration, and Irritability

We may not get human communication right on many levels (and we'll get into how to address this!) but once we add a layer of

Effectiveness Through Managing Workplace Emotion

technological intermediation like email, chat, or even video, things can really go haywire. One wild piece of research estimated "miscommunication rates" at 87% for email, 80% for text, 79% for online chat (like Slack or Teams), 71% for phone calls, and 67% for voicemail.[7] After I got past my natural first question (Who leaves voicemails? Is that still an option?), I have to say this resonated. After all, I had gotten two fairly terrible emails in the 2 hours before reading the research. And I'm not sure the ones I sent in response were any good, either, to be fair to my email correspondents.

And that's just the impact of technology on communication. Then there's technology on its own, and what child and adolescent psychiatrist Dr. Ross Goodwin calls "technostress."[8] Goodwin breaks the stress of technology into three categories: "techno-overload" (when technology is just too much); "techno-complexity" (when technological change means you need new skills at work); and "techno-invasion" (when technology means your work intrudes more into your life). Each of the three, in their own way, help drive negative emotions—either feelings of overwhelm, confusion, or frustration. Remember the last time you were really psyched to get five chat pings at once while sitting on your sofa at 10 at night? Me neither.

Scale and Complexity Are Doing Us No Favors Here, Either

Let's come back to our Middle Ages example. If you worked on a farm in 1300, you knew most of the other folks on the farm. You might never leave your small village where you also knew everyone. As a consequence, while you might not like everyone, you got fairly familiar with folks' communication styles and the general context of their lives. In contrast, let's say you're you today—and you work in a decently complex organization, or even a pretty large company, with lots of "teams of teams." You may often work with the same people, but you're also challenged to collaborate with folks you know a little bit or don't know at all. You may not be a jerk—in fact you probably

Effective

aren't a jerk—but the potential for conflict has just escalated massively, because you don't know folks as well.

We're in a Listening Crisis

I interviewed a diverse array of folks for this book, and this was perhaps the major theme that emerged across some very different conversations. Dustin Liu, the Senior Associate Director of the NYU Stern Initiative on Purpose and Flourishing, told me how "We're communicating more and we're sharing updates, but we're not actually holding space for conversations that may actually shift your perception of someone's needs." In a similar vein, UVA professor Jim Detert passionately described how "So often, my advice is to talk less and listen more—actually hear something people different from us say and not immediately write it off as ridiculous." Consulting leader and private equity executive Michelle Stuntz even asserts that "listening to the unwritten rules of the environment you're in—the things that no one is going to tell you—can ward off a lot of chaos." (More on that in Chapter 9.)

How Emotional Workplaces Affect Our Effectiveness Architecture

Excessively emotional workplaces can feel incredibly draining. But interestingly, they affect different parts of our Effectiveness Architecture quite differently. Let's take a look.

Emotional Workplaces and Knowledge: Impact Level 3/10

If your area of strength within the Effectiveness Architecture is Knowledge, congratulations: in an emotional workplace, you get to be the eye of the storm. You may suffer through some emotionally inflected back and forth about facts that are, in your mind, quite clear—but, in general, folks who are strong in Knowledge occupy a place of calm amidst emotional turmoil at work. You generally don't see subject matter experts pulled into shouting matches unless their area of expertise comes under direct fire.

Emotional Workplaces and Methods: Impact Level 7/10

Emotional workplaces have a sneakily corrosive impact on Methods, making every interaction more charged and thus causing systemic slowdowns and stoppages across what should be uncontroversial workflows. If you're a real Methods fiend, folks in an emotionally aroused state may actually get frustrated with you, and it's understandable; there's nothing more irritating than someone "just trying to get things done" when you're truly upset.

Emotional Workplaces and People: Impact Level 10/10

If your strength is People, emotionally charged workplaces will challenge you severely for an interesting reason: you'll get serially called in to fix the most emotional situations. People is only a secondary strength for me, but I've experienced a version of this phenomenon in my career. Folks came to my office—physically or virtually—to cry. I got assigned notably tough clients because I could handle their emotional outbursts. I became a shock absorber for anger, sadness, disappointment . . . you name it. It's damn near impossible to be effective under those conditions, and of course your own mental health suffers too. (Later in this chapter, Dr. Rebecca Parker has some great guidance on how to handle being a co-worker's shoulder to cry on, in a way that's humane to them and to you.)

Emotional Workplaces and Technology: Impact Level 2/10

Similar to Knowledge, if your area of strength within the Effectiveness Architecture is Technology, you're a bit outside the fray of emotional workplaces. You'll want to be watchful that you're not making technology choices that accidentally heighten emotions.

And to that end, let's look at the specific example of folks who work in customer service—because there are interesting lessons there for us all about emotions in a world of fast technological evolution.

Canaries in the Coal Mine: What We Can Learn About Humans, Technology, and Emotion from the Struggles of Customer Service

When was the last time you called customer service? May I ask how it went?

The bad news is that you probably had a rocky moment or two. And the other bad news is that if you did interact with a human being, they may not have enjoyed that interaction very much either.

As per the data from our April 2025 study—and a host of other studies—customer service is having a moment, and it's not a good one. One scientific article on call center workers in India, for instance, paints a pretty rough picture:

> *Call center employees are expected to express positive emotions and suppress negative emotions like frustration, resentment, and anger, in their interactions with customers so as to create a desired state of mind in the customer. If not given a healthy expressive outlet, this emotional repression can profoundly affect a person psychologically.*[9]

The same article cites studies observing everything from insomnia to addictions to physical ailments at highly elevated levels among call center populations. A diet of constant negative emotion is making folks sick—literally.

What's fascinating about where customer service roles have ended up is that we've actually gotten here through a series of what seemed to be constructive or at least neutral choices, often involving deploying technological advances. To better understand what happened—and to hopefully avoid the same for other roles—let's walk through these changes.

It's not a new idea that companies would want any task performed at the lowest possible cost. But until relatively recently—say, the last few decades—that was difficult to do. There might be cheaper labor a few towns over, but the office was in this town, and what were you going to do, stay on the phone with each other all day? That would be pure folly.

With the advent of the Internet and a host of other tools to manage and transmit data, suddenly organizations had far more choices. We immediately think of globalization as the choice that got made, shifting customer service (and other functions) offshore. But even with some elements of cross-cultural clash, globalization is not the major driver of heightened emotions in the customer service arena.

Technology is.

To think about how technology has both helped customer service personnel and potentially harmed them, consider what might be even lower cost than a human: technology *operated by your own customer*. The cheapest labor for any organization is the person buying things from you—they're not just not taking your money, they're giving you theirs! What's sometimes terrific is that customers might want to do the work themselves. I like placing my own coffee order on an app. I like doing simple debugging of my router on my cable company's app. We all buy so many things without ever speaking to a salesperson. It's often easier and simpler to be our own customer service . . . and, in general, we like it.

So, what's going wrong? Complexity and ambiguity, that's what.

Effective

Consider the examples I just shared. None of them are rocket science. Even your craziest raspberry matcha cold foam triple macchiato order boils down to a series of simple choices (many of them gross in my mind, but you do you! Get the boba pearls if that's your bliss!). The second things get complex, today's technology starts to tap out. One simple example: voice chatbots. Just tell the chatbot verbally what you want, right? Well, if mumble a bit (me), have a slight accent (my husband), or have a higher voice (my daughter), the chatbot may not understand you. If your question is not something standard, the chatbot may not understand you. If the proscribed pathways that the chatbot moves you through don't pan out, the chatbot may not know what to do. Eventually, after a lot of "SPEAK. To a HUMAN" you're back on the phone with a human employee.

But think about how you feel at that moment. You feel not heard and not understood. You may have raised your voice. You may be getting one of those back-of-the-skull blood pressure headaches. You're not in good shape.

Now imagine you're the customer service representative. You get a whole string of that shouting person with the blood pressure headache all day long. You don't have to work in a call center to get there—you might be in a drug store and the self-checkout just failed someone. You might be in a coffee shop and the kiosk conked out. The common thread is, you have to come in and clean up for a technology that could not fulfill human expectations.

That's emotionally charged work. We all need to consider—could our job be heading there? It sounds wonderful to automate the most basic aspects of work—and it *eventually* always is. But the middle distance can be a hairball. I imagine the horse and buggy driver who had to come pick up folks whose Model T broke down on the outskirts of town probably had some interesting customer service interactions too.

Effectiveness Through Managing Workplace Emotion

So, here are a few thought questions about effectiveness in emotional workplaces that you can take away from what we're already seeing in customer service:

- *Does my job in any way follow up on a technological layer that may have failed?* If so—be ready to communicate empathically with the person who dealt with the imperfect technology (customer or co-worker alike). But also give yourself a break: you do not need to be the sacrificial lamb for every misplaced bit or byte. What's interesting is that you can be a relatively senior executive and still get whacked by others' bad experience of technology; trying to deal with buggy performance management systems at year end is an excellent example of this phenomenon.

- *Where I am making a choice to deploy technology in my day-to-day work, have I adequately anticipated the emotional impact it may have?* For instance, there's a hot debate in entrepreneurial circles about scheduling apps. I have one; I use it sparingly. Being asked to use a scheduling app drives some people squarely up the wall—especially in the scenario where someone contacts you and then asks you to use their app to schedule with them. I get this; it has the feel of the old cartoon with a guy telling a bookstore employee: "I'd like to buy a book on chutzpah and I'd like you to pay for it."[10] You called me! Why are you asking me to do the scheduling work for you? It's a great example of a seemingly neutral technology choice stirring up unwanted emotion. It's critical to watch out for these.

- *When is a situation so emotionally fraught that I should not use technology at all?* I resigned from a job once and was told to call

Effective

a shared services number to formalize my departure. Okay, cool. So, I get to one of those automated menus. "For retirement accounts, press 1. For benefits, press 2. To resign, press 3." To resign, press 3? Really folks? For weeks, I told this story to everyone who would listen. I couldn't believe it. Then it got worse! For a real estate purchase, I needed some documentation of a retirement account from another prior employer. Their menu options came through as follows: "For benefits, press 1. For retirement accounts, press 2. To report a death, press 3." To report a death? I do not want to press a number to report a death! To be fair, I've had a number of clients in the insurance industry and that industry has gotten well sensitized to the issue over the years, given the emotionally fraught nature of their business. It's not uncommon for an insurance company to designate customer no-fly zones where only human voices are heard and virtually no automation is used. We should all look at our technology choices similarly thoughtfully—with a sharp eye toward the emotion they provoke.

Managing Emotion in the Workplace: Practical Strategies for Different Scenarios

So, here we are, dealing with workplace anger, sadness, and stress, some of it accidentally caused by otherwise sound technological choices, and some of it just a function of a challenging and complex world. What can we do? What are our strategies for managing this third dimension of work intensification?

Let's look at some different scenarios where emotion might be running high and think about how you can be effective despite their challenges.

Effectiveness Through Managing Workplace Emotion

Scenario 1: Someone Just Blew Up at Me

There's an iconic scene in the 1976 movie *Network* in which anchorman Howard Beale, in full meltdown in the wake of his show's cancellation, yells "I'm mad as hell and I'm not going to take it anymore![11] The scene became an instant classic because, while most of us will hopefully not experience a mental health crisis of Beale's magnitude, the underlying sentiment of accrued frustration does resonate across so many jobs. We don't melt down out of the blue; we explode, as UVA professor Jim Detert explains, after many cycles of failed communication. Detert narrates what's often going on in someone's head as they start screaming: "I tried to bring this issue up multiple times and I did it in a very calm way. I offered data. I was reasonable and you kept ignoring it, and so finally my level of frustration got to the point where I didn't communicate it very skillfully. Anger tends to have a real reason."

Detert is offering a great reframe here: instead of seeing a messy meltdown, see someone trying to communicate something important who hasn't been heard historically, and thus isn't doing it perfectly. Focus on making them feel heard *now*, and the emotional temperature should start to come down. And, of course, where you can, try to make folks heard earlier in the cycle. I often counsel leaders to not block out what they perceive as "whiny" input from their teams . . . you may be hearing something that (1) the person will eventually melt down about and (2) is important and you should act on. If you find yourself starting to dismiss "whiny" statements, remind yourself that it's just data. It's information. You can act on it or not, but don't dismiss it out of hand. There's no downside, too, to making people feel heard.

Scenario 2: Someone's in Tears (or Tears-Adjacent)

The movie quote for this one is obviously *A League of Their Own*'s "There's no crying in baseball!"[12] Plenty of crying in business unfortunately—and it's unfairly stigmatized. Similar to scenario 1, shutting down your own "inflammatory response"—the inner voice that says that people who cry are wimps/useless/immature—should be your first step. Reframe as "this person's emotional state is manifesting itself physically," or something like that. One person's tears might be another person's stooped shoulders . . . our bodies all work differently.

Then, figure out your own role. They might just need you to listen—as Dr. Rebecca Parker observes, when we experience tough stuff at work, we need an "anchor" to absorb it. But then—as she also notes—you've taken on the negative emotion yourself. And you too will need an anchor of your own—you can't just absorb bad feelings into your own body and hope for the best. If the crying person needs action, one interesting point of recourse might be the Knowledge portion of your Effectiveness Architecture. With all that fast-moving organizational complexity that we talked about at the beginning of the chapter, it's not uncommon for folks to be despondent based on completely incorrect information (e.g., "I heard there will be no promotions or raises this year!"). Start by just making sure they have all of their facts right. Often that makes a dent in their negative emotion quickly.

Scenario 3: The Team Is Constantly at War with Itself

If you'll permit me a bit of latitude with the war metaphor here, your first step should be to destroy the battlefield. Are people fighting on an email chain? End it. A Teams chat? Redirect it (don't shut the entire chat down—that starts to look strange). A staff meeting? If you can, reconfigure the meeting or get some subteams meeting on particular issues. Your goal here is to force a refresh for the folks actually fighting—and to eliminate spectators. Big meetings, email chains, and chats can take on a "Christians and lions in the arena" dynamic,

Effectiveness Through Managing Workplace Emotion

where a few combatants are watched (and implicitly egged on) by a large, silent audience. The spectators aren't helping, and everyone needs a break, so the quicker you can get rid of the conflict arena, the better.

Next, get the smaller group of combatants into a virtual room, and facilitate some constructive disagreement. Set down good rules of the road, like no *ad hominems* (personal insults). For this to work, you have to actually let them disagree without constantly interfering, which is quite difficult for many leaders trained to avoid conflict like the plague. You also have to listen for "the issues behind the issues"—which you may or may not be able to solve in the room.

Scenario 4: I'm Getting Emotional Myself

Let me make a surprising statement here: this may not be a bad thing. As per Jim Detert from UVA's research, *as long as people perceive you as being in control of your emotions*, emotion in the workplace is just fine—and often appropriate. It's weird not to be sad when something terrible happens. It's weird not to be happy when there's a resounding success. And so on. People only perceive emotion as inappropriate when it seems that you don't have your emotions in hand. Accordingly, it's helpful to go take a walk around the block, or have a candid conversation with your "anchor," but you shouldn't get yourself down to a level of robotic impassivity, which then starts to read as inauthentic and credibility-destroying. Emote in a well-regulated fashion, and you're more effective than a colleague who stays poker-faced.

As Chapter 7 Comes to a Close . . .

So, as we bring Chapter 7 to a close, let's talk about how we get started on the journey of being effective even when workplace emotions are running high.

Effective

For everyone

- *Take some great advice from UVA professor Jim Detert—use evolutionary cues to nonverbally "read the room."* When Detert mentioned to me in our interview that people often miss body language cues and misread others' emotions, I asked him to give me a little more detail on what they should look for. Evolutionary science is the key, he told me. If someone is sitting with their arms or legs crossed, or their body angled away or hunched, they're mimicking an ancestor from thousands of years ago who might have protected their body from physical harm that way. Similarly, if their feet seem glued to the floor, from an evolutionary standpoint they are making themselves ready to run from danger. Even on video calls, many of these movements are readily visible. Picking up on discomfort that's expressed nonverbally can be a great step toward making sure negative emotions don't surge in any given interaction.

- *To keep emotional temperatures down, speak less.* Back to that theme around the listening crisis—if the listening crisis got us into this emotional pickle, the way out is generally through . . . listening. But as Detert, Liu, McDonald, and a host of others pointed out, definitionally to listen you have to stop speaking first. Dr. Rebecca Parker cites a neat statistic from research conducted in the medical field: the vast majority of patients will tell you what's wrong with them, or give you the information to readily discern it, within 90 seconds, given the chance. But that requires 90 full seconds of you not speaking. Try it: time 90 seconds of silence to see what it feels like. It'll feel like an eternity for most folks. That's the kind of silence you need for people to tell you important things—and feel emotionally satisfied with the conversation as a result.

Effectiveness Through Managing Workplace Emotion

If you're the boss

- *Map out where things are getting emotional for your team using the 5 Ws: Who, What, When, Where, Why.* At the risk of making you feel like you're back at your high school newspaper, the 5 Ws really are the best way to look at emotionally charged trouble spots for your team—with an eye toward addressing them. Are there particular folks with a higher emotional valence? (This isn't a negative, it's just a thing that is.) Are there particular subjects or underlying thematics that trigger emotion? (Times of year?) (Year end and comp time may feature prominently.) Particular "locations?" (Hint: specific meetings.) Knowing where things repeatedly get emotional is the first step toward navigating to a more peaceful way of working.

- *Audit how you yourself are using emotion with your team.* Coming back to Jim Detert's research finding that showing that emotion is properly harnessed is the key to productive leader–team interactions, take a look at your own use of emotion across a couple of weeks at work. Are you generally expressing positive or negative emotions? (No right answer per se, but a balance is often appropriate.) Are you generally expressing yourself in a measured manner, or do you feel out of control at times? If you have peers who can give you feedback—ask them—are you showing emotional control?

If you're the big boss

- *Take a searching look at the emotional landscape of your organization—including customers, partners, and other outside stakeholders.* Make sure you look "beyond the ivory tower." When it comes to emotional workplaces, the very nature of organizations often shields executives from the full nature of what's going on—good or bad. You'll want to put on your detective hat and look for clues. Engagement survey data or social media representations of your company (yes, steel yourself and open Glassdoor!) may contain interesting representations of where emotion is flaring, and where it's well channeled. A bit of "mystery shopper"—or *Undercover Boss* if you remember that TV show—work may be in order, too. Understanding firsthand the emotions experienced by your frontline workers, particularly as they interact with customers, can be key to a host of smarter business decisions. Negative, spiraling emotion may be chipping away at profitability—silently drawing energy away from the things your organization truly wants to accomplish. Conversely, if there are places where emotions (positive or negative) are being harnessed adeptly, that's a wonderful case study to replicate more broadly.

Emotion in the workplace can be a gnarly challenge. So, let's move on to an even gnarlier one: hyper-transparent workplaces. When everyone "knows" everything—and everyone has access to "everything" (air quotes deliberate in both cases), work gets really tricky really fast . . . but also gets a lot better in certain ways, too.

Hyper transparency is a fascinating workplace trend because unlike the others we've looked at (work intensification, emotional workplaces) or will look at (chaos), it truly cuts both ways. Treated properly, it can help make you, your team, and your organization more effective. Handled unintentionally, it can impede the very building blocks of effectiveness.

Let's go down both rabbit holes.

Effectiveness Through Managing Workplace Emotion

Chapter 8

Effectiveness Through Harnessing Transparency Properly

Let me take this moment to set the record straight: I did not rig the employee engagement awards.

Stop laughing! A few years ago, this was a real thing that I believed I was being accused of. And the whole tale of woe starts to give us some interesting insight into the challenges of working in today's hyper-transparent workplaces—including how our own psychology can get tricky.

Before we get into why no one's going to ask me to host the Oscars anytime soon, let's talk about what it means for workplaces to be more transparent today than they have been for a while historically, and why that might affect your effectiveness. We've got a few things all going on at once:

- *Data-driven organizations.* Incredible effort has been spent over the last decades on better capturing key information, analyzing it, and making it more visible to more people inside companies.

- *Changing regulation on pay transparency.* In the United States, 14 states and Washington DC have now enacted laws requiring some sort of disclosure on what folks in particular roles actually earn.[1]

- *Social media.* Company rating site Glassdoor, alone, reports 63 million unique visitors *a month.*[2] And that's just one work-specific venue for discussion: of course, we talk about work on every other social media tool, from long, detailed discussions on Reddit to 15-second skits on TikTok.

- *Internal communication tools.* Who needs a watercooler when you have 15 zillion group chats—both on company-sponsored platforms like Slack and Teams, as well as personal ones like text messaging and WhatsApp?

All these factors combine to form today's hyper-transparent workplace. Lots of information floats around; everyone talks about everything. More data and more information, of varying quality, is available to more people—inside and outside the company. You don't have to be a world-famous company to have a very active and live external dialogue—for instance, the smallest company in the Fortune 500, Vulcan Materials, has more than 500 Glassdoor reviews.[3] It's hard to even capture the velocity of companies' internal communications today, but consider that one platform—Slack—handles 1.5 *billion* messages every workday.[4]

Simply put, there are just many, many more conversations about and at work than ever before.

One result: hyper-transparent workplaces feature some seismic shifts in power dynamics. As I noted in my *MIT Sloan Management Review* article, "Leading in the Age of Exploding Transparency": "technology is meaningfully eroding the information advantage leaders have enjoyed since the dawn of the working world."[5] If you're a leader who practices "mushroom management" ("keep 'em in the dark and feed them lots of manure"[6]), you may struggle with how well lit things are these days . . . though luckily for you, manure still seems to be in good supply.

Hyper-transparent workplaces definitely challenge our effectiveness in a whole bunch of ways that I'll get into shortly, but first it's worth noting: they're not a universally negative phenomenon.

Effective

Unlike work intensification or overly emotional workplaces (Chapters 6 and 7) or chaos (Chapter 9), transparency at work has the potential to be a wholly good thing when addressed properly. We're just at the "baby steps" stage of doing so.

So, let's return, with a sigh, to one of the cringier moments of my professional career—and look at how struggles around transparency play out in the real world.

It was one of those incidents where a whole bunch of good intentions added up in a messy way. In challenging times, leadership had decided to recognize some folks for their contributions to company culture, as chosen by nominations and popular vote. It was a good concept, and the awards were well framed (things like "the Unsung Hero"). A couple of senior folks in my reporting chain then decided to concretely campaign for their team, which was also a nice idea—making sure folks' contributions got recognized. Separately, I was asked to emcee, which I was thrilled to do. All good things.

During the actual awards ceremony, though, things got awkward. Folks from my group kept winning—and although I knew it was for very normal reasons (people being organized about asking for votes), my anxious mind couldn't escape the feeling that it looked suspicious. I made a crack about how well I'd done at rigging the voting process. It was the only thing I could think of to do to diffuse the tension (that I myself felt).

Imagine my horror, then, when I took a look at the consulting industry app Fishbowl the next day, and saw a whole discussion around a lack of diversity in the award recipients, including the following commentary:

There is inherent bias in whoever organizes this and the folks that are in those organizers' circles . . . appear more prominently. The whole approach is flawed, and you can

Effectiveness Through Harnessing Transparency

Yikes. At this point my already anxious brain went into full meltdown. I read this as them taking literally my quip about rigging the awards.

I was being unjustly accused! I didn't even help organize the darn thing; I just showed up and riffed off a script like a typical useless corporate executive! How could I be guilty of these crimes when I didn't even really help with anything in the first place? And as I kept telling people at the time, if I actually had the ability and the diminished moral sense to rig the firm's internal processes, would it not be compensation or promotions that I'd monkey with? I mean, come on, go big or go home!

With the help of time, diminished emotion, looking at other posts for context, and deploying an elementary school level of reading comprehension, I now realize . . . that's not what they were trying to say.

The point of the posts was that recognition could be a bit of a closed system, when handled improperly. From the outside, it looked like a small group of people put together the awards and put a lot of effort into making sure their closest contacts won them.

That wasn't the reality (again, I was just a talking head!), but I can now absolutely see why that was their perception of the situation. There was some truth to that view, in a way: as long as a relatively small group of folks approached the awards with greater engagement than others, the results might end up looking skewed. This was a useful, fair challenge to management. My freakout was unjustified.

It genuinely pained me to type out that story—it was cringey then and it's cringey now, for totally different reasons. But I think it

Effective

highlights some fundamental truths about operating in more transparent workplaces that it serves us well to acknowledge:

1. *My obvious is different from yours.* From my vantage point, it was obvious that I had no control over the awards. I'd had the process explained several times and I'd had a leader's eye view of how it progressed. But from the point of view of someone not in leadership, it would seem apparent that the person presenting the information would have been involved in putting the awards together. It's not the right conclusion, but it's a totally logical one. Wrong "obvious"es happen all the time—particularly when an organization goes silent on a topic that's important to an employee. "Obviously I'm not getting promoted." No, we're just 3 weeks late making congratulations calls because we're waiting for a final approval! The human brain's inclination to interpret the absence of facts negatively does a lot of nasty work here.

2. *When information comes through an unexpected channel, it's hard to process.* Logically, then, as a leader in consulting, I've had more conversations than I could count correcting reasonable, well-intentioned misinterpretations of the facts. I'm happy to have these conversations and I've learned to be very emotionally modulated about them, as I've understood better and better how people get their hands on odd versions of the truth. I'll be candid here, though: I wasn't prepared, emotionally, to read about myself on social media. Not one bit. In a more transparent world, you may hear the same news through a channel you did not anticipate in at all—and that may really throw you. I've seen leaders become apoplectic when their direct reports contacted that leader's boss without going through their own manager first—a direct function, I believe, of a "flatter" world facilitated by the use

Effectiveness Through Harnessing Transparency

of email. You might not have called your boss's boss—you almost certainly would not have booked a meeting with them—but you're often going to feel a lot less inhibited about just dropping them a quick email. Which means your boss hears about you being upset not from you, but from the leader above them. It's not hard to see how this can spur some not-so-positive reactions. Again, what's triggering is not the information itself, but the channel it came through. As consulting leader and private equity executive Michelle Stuntz notes, it can be disconcerting to hear information from a person you didn't expect or in a sequence you didn't expect—even if the information itself is banal enough.

3. *More transparency = greater emphasis on the "how."* Part of what goes on in more transparent organizations is that *expectations change.* I've watched expectations shift during my own career. When I was a mid-level consultant at a Big 4 firm back in the day, I didn't have massive expectations around understanding how decisions got made or processes ran. By the time I hit consulting leadership, folks at mid level routinely approached me with just these questions. This isn't a "kids these days"—this is a changed world, where more overall transparency (or, as we'll get into, the appearance of more transparency!) has shifted folks' beliefs on what information can and should be shared. Hence the discussion in the awards instance: people were (rightly!) interested in how the sausage got made, including the nitty gritty of who ran the process and who it rewarded. This is a more challenging conversation but ultimately a positive one. I believe in the cliché that sunlight is the best disinfectant—that transparency can improve underlying conditions—and we'll talk more in this chapter about the not-always-comfortable process to make that happen.

Effective

How Hyper-Transparency Hits Your Effectiveness Architecture

Most of us don't routinely consider how transparency at work is affecting our effectiveness. That is, in part, because its impact on the Effectiveness Architecture is fairly uneven. Let's see what that looks like.

Hyper-Transparency and Knowledge: Impact Level 5/10

If Knowledge is your area of strength within the Effectiveness Architecture, hyper-transparent environments are quite a mixed blessing. On the one hand, they're full of your favorite thing: facts about stuff! Hyper-transparent environments can really allow Knowledge-oriented folks to blossom, since there's so much emphasis on exchanging information. On the other hand, and this is the rub: not all facts are as fact-y as other facts. Hyper-transparent environments, with a lot of information coming through the pipes, are unfortunately prone to not just information overload—but misinformation overload. Knowledge-oriented folks can find this highly triggering.

Hyper-Transparency and Methods: Impact Level 3/10

For Methods-driven folks, hyper-transparency doesn't have a huge impact. There is some skill involved in getting things done in information-rich environments—marshalling folks who are constantly communicating—but this skill tends to already be an arrow in the quiver of people who are good at Methods. They may experience moments of frustration at the constant back and forth that goes on, but in general, hyper-transparency just ups the game of Methods-oriented people.

Effectiveness Through Harnessing Transparency

Hyper-Transparency and People: Impact Level 8/10

This one's got a good movie quote: "You can't handle the truth!" Perhaps the most potent negative impact of hyper-transparency—and one we'll talk about a lot in this chapter—is dealing with folks' reactions to information they either do not want to hear at all, or think they want to hear then cannot handle. While folks who are strong in the People part of the Effectiveness Architecture are best equipped to handle these crises, similar to dealing with emotional workplaces the process can be incredibly draining for them.

Hyper-Transparency and Technology: Impact Level 1/10

Folks who excel at the Technology portion of the Effectiveness Architecture have a bit of a super-power in hyper-transparent environments. Their skills around navigating the many systems, apps, and technologies in play position them well to do things like parse out what information is accurate and what's inaccurate and utilize communications technology with grace, even as many conversations go at once.

Hyper-Transparency: Handling Some Increasingly Common Scenarios

Hyper-transparency can sound a bit abstract, but the reality is that it plays out in some very common, repeated scenarios. Have a look at the following and see if any of them sound familiar.

Bad News Got Communicated Accidentally, Not Intentionally

In Chapter 5, we heard from emergency room physician Dr. Rebecca Parker about the high level of intentionality that doctors use to communicate bad news to patients' loved ones. Every profession has a version of this, but today's hyper-transparent workplaces are more prone than ever to "leaks." Whether you're a leader or working at the frontline, having bad news slip out without the proper context and framing—internally or, worse, externally—can feel nightmarish.

What to do: Target your audience with precision and lead with evidence *in context.* With bad news running amok, your temptation may be to set the record straight universally—to get the truth to as many folks as possible as quickly as possible. Resist this impulse. Instead, choose the stakeholders for whom the correct framing is most important, and use your energy to communicate with them first and foremost. There's no right formula for who this would be (internal vs. external, senior vs. junior, small circle vs. mass audience)—the right answer is situationally specific. Then, make sure this group gets two things: data/evidence and, critically, context. Ferrovial CIO Dimitris Bountolos explains the care and precision this takes:

> *You have to aggregate and disaggregate information to make sure that everyone has the right context to avoid creating ripple effects of chaos. You're trying to avoid someone amplifying what is irrelevant, magnifying noise over signal, or worst of all, creating a different perspective of reality entirely.*

Remember that in this instance, restoring context (which has almost certainly gotten lost) is just as important as reasserting the facts. All too often, people get two sets of facts and compare them improperly, picking the less true set as more intuitively apparent. Context helps them actually make sense of the information they're given and will steer folks back to the right message quicker.

Effectiveness Through Harnessing Transparency

The Rumor Mill Spins Overtime

Hello, and welcome to every place I've ever worked! Rumor mills have long been a sad fact of corporate life, amplified meaningfully in recent decades by contemporary technologies like email, chat, and text messaging. One academic study found that a breathtaking 90% of office discussions contained gossip; another study noted that people spend 52 minutes a day on gossip.[8,9] Both sets of research reached the rather obvious conclusion that positive gossip was good for individuals and the businesses they worked for, and negative gossip was, in contrast, quite toxic for both people and organizations.

What to do: Find a sensible place in the gossip ecosystem and do some real-time fact checking. A generation ago, you could just stay away from the water cooler and keep your nose in your own knitting, so to speak. In a hyper-transparent workplace, with rumors flying every which way, it's not sensible at any level to fully insulate yourself for what might be, in some cases, useful information coming to you through an informal channel. At the same time, given the clear data on the negative impacts of negative gossip—and given the fact that actually-true-truth is ever more valuable in a deepfake world—you do not want to be the self-appointed Page Six of your organization. A good positioning might be, "I am open to hearing what's going on, but I'm pretty passionate about the facts." Be a bit of a nudge (I'm pronouncing that "noodge") about where folks' information actually comes from, and of course be incredibly selective about the fact quality (and implications) of what you pass on. Similar to office politics, office gossip isn't something any of us can fully stay out of, but we don't want to get mired in it either.

Bonus tip: Leaders in particular often miss an opportunity to shut down rumors: keeping a stream of communication going even when

Effective

there's no new "news" to pass on. Mary Cianni explains how, throughout her career, she's counseled clients in difficult, sensitive situations around mergers or acquisitions:

One of the things that I always pushed our clients to do is if there's nothing new then say that there's nothing new. If there's a period of silence people fill in the blanks with negative stories they concoct in their own heads. So transparency is also just saying we haven't made any decisions or we're moving on this decision but we can't share that information.

Consulting leader and private equity executive Michelle Stuntz saw the same in a high-pressure private equity environment:

Responsiveness in communication goes a long way to keeping people calm. People fill the void. So, the more there are voids where you aren't providing what you want them to know, that's when they begin to invent information and worry.

Human nature is actually to assume that no news is bad news, but leaders can actively mitigate this tendency by being clear that no news is, in fact, no news.

New Data Has Become Available and Its Meaning Is Not Yet Fully Clear/Is Disputed

The promise of the data-driven organization is a fabulous one: everyone has access to excellent information, quantified and analyzed, and on that basis, all decisions are good decisions, because they're

Effectiveness Through Harnessing Transparency

fact-based. Sadly, we have not quite arrived at this utopian state yet. Many organizations are at a suboptimal point right now: awash in data of hugely varying quality and veracity, often struggling with big-picture meaning. In my own career, I've been part of teams that—despite decent data availability—have wrestled with what would seem like quite basic questions: "Is this group sufficiently engaged or not?" "Is this work ultimately profitable?" And so on. The availability of data sometimes massively fore-runs the ability of that data to help us make sense of running a business. In a data-rich environment, we make the mistake of going after numbers, not answers, as HR executive and organizational consultant Thiago Licias de Oliveira notes: "The key challenge isn't access—it's judgment. People chase data without clarity on the problem they're solving or the opportunity they're pursuing." It's also increasingly unclear what's the right data to share. Axialent partner Teryluz Andreu explains how this often plays out in dealing with people data (like pay, job architecture, or performance ratings):

Do you want to lean more into transparency, meaning communicating very openly what you can expect as you move through different jobs, or are you going to let people just reach their own inferences in terms of what's going on? They can, after all, go to different sources of data and reach their own conclusions, wrong or right.

What to do: Don't take data at face value—take it apart methodically and in a contextualized fashion. Think like a data scientist or a detective—whichever identity you prefer. In my *MIT Sloan Management Review* article "Four Leadership Loads that Keep Getting Heavier," I describe this process:

[Ask] better questions of information, in a structured and methodical way. Don't be afraid to ask where data came

from, what the gaps in a data set might be, or what kinds of analytics were performed to get to the numbers you're seeing. Come in with a hypothesis and see if it proves out rather than just taking the numbers at face value. It's slightly counterintuitive, but being a tougher data analyst makes you a better truth sleuth.[10]

One great example of the complexity behind a single data point comes from the realm of pay transparency. Tauseef Rahman explains that by the time a pay range is posted in a job listing, "that's so many steps into the process." Sitting behind that single pay range are a whole set of decisions and assumptions on everything from how hard it is to be a senior marketing manager to what it costs to live in Minneapolis to what the organization's underlying philosophy on pay even *is*.

It's easy to see a number and have a quick reaction, but it's worth taking the time to unpack how someone got to that number . . . and whether it's even accurate at all. I recently had a hair-raising encounter with a financial services customer service representative who insisted passionately that I was leaving a life-changing amount of money on the table by switching investments . . . while mistakenly quoting me the yearly payoff as a monthly one! I told him to follow up with the math in writing, leading to a sheepish email where he admitted the mistake. This sort of simple "that doesn't make sense, can you clarify where you got the data?" move is incredibly valuable in a world where so many folks are reading a decontextualized number out of a box (and feeling mistakenly confident in it).

Social Media Has Entered the Chat

Try though we might to set some clear guardrails, social media has, in many workplaces, become an integral part of how we work.

Effectiveness Through Harnessing Transparency

The most comprehensive study on the subject was conducted back in 2016 by the Pew Center.[11] Even then, usage levels were impressively high: 1 in 5 folks surveyed were actually using social media at work *for* work (to find problem-solving information); roughly 1 in 8 were using it to ask work-related questions of people outside their organization; and a similar proportion were using it to ask work-related questions of people inside their organization. Amusingly, in 14% of cases social media raised people's opinions of co-workers, and 16% of the time it lowered their opinions!

What to do: When it comes to work and social media, be simple in how you show up, but also focused in how you search for information on others. Saying that social media is a smoke-and-mirrors world is hugely unfair to smoke and mirrors. It's messy and often dishonest out there, and not in a way that any individual can solve. What we can do is represent ourselves clearly, inasmuch as that's humanly possible, and avoid going down rabbit holes on others . . . in as much as that's humanly possible. Back to that statistic about social media lowering our opinions of our co-workers 16% of the time: it's rare to hear that someone learned a fact about a co-worker on social media that changed their opinion for the better. More often, we end up either feeling weird and uncomfortable ("did not need to see that guy's beach photos!") or actually ethically challenged in some way (e.g., when folks' educational credentials turn out to not be exactly what they verbally claimed, a not uncommon scenario). So, stay out of the rabbit hole if you can, and curate your own online presence smartly too. You may want to make accounts with personal or political content private—similar to how you wouldn't invite many co-workers into your home or argue politics with them in real life.

Transparency: Finding and Maximizing the Upside

Before I even had a chance to interview him, my former Mercer colleague Tauseef Rahman emailed me a really well-framed thought on the subject of pay transparency:

> *Pay transparency gets framed as the problem, when the real underlying problems are systemic inequities and a lack of understanding of the differences in jobs, the determinants of pay, etc. Pay transparency doesn't cause issues or misunderstandings, it exposes them.*

This is a great way to think about transparency, period, beyond just the pay realm. The issue isn't transparency itself, it's the underlying problems it brings to light. Which means there's a huge amount of upside possible: if you can name what's wrong, you're that much closer to fixing it . . . even if that moment of seeing and naming the issue is deeply uncomfortable. More broadly, getting information to circulate in a sensible fashion is a wonderful dimension of effectiveness—both for those of us passionate about the Knowledge part of the Effectiveness Architecture, and for the rest of y'all. As Flipkart president and board advisor Vipin Gupta notes:

> *Transparency makes behaviors like cross-functional decision-making much smoother. And cross-functional decisions are the real driver of organizational agility. Truly agile organizations focus on managing decisions, not tasks.*

Effectiveness Through Harnessing Transparency

So, let's dive into the upside of transparency—and look at ways that we can all become more effective in a world that can feel like information overload.

Be the Person Who Gets the Bad News in Time to Do Something About It . . . and Then Do Something About It

Former Clorox Chief Supply Chain Officer (CSCO) Rick McDonald has a saying, "Good news fast, bad news faster." Throughout his career, he's focused on creating a leadership climate where people will tell him if something is going wrong as quickly as possible, maximizing the chance that he'll be able to fix the problem in a timely fashion.

This really resonates—missed opportunities to stave off big problems fascinate me. David McCullough's eponymous book about the catastrophic Johnstown flood, for example, contains a poignant example of a failed attempt to communicate to the townspeople of Johnstown the true level of danger from a dam break, as rain came down in ominous quantities on May 31, 1889. A telegraph message came in stating the facts quite clearly:

SOUTH FORK DAM IS LIABLE TO BREAK: NOTIFY THE PEOPLE OF JOHNSTOWN TO PREPARE FOR THE WORST.[12]

As communications go, this is a pretty good one: terse, simple, urgent. But no one did anything about it: one freight agent talked to a few people, one of whom actually laughed. No one shared the message more broadly or acted on it. As a result, more than 2,000 people died, and in today's terms, hundreds of millions of dollars in damage were incurred.[13]

This is the sort of scenario—preventable destruction—that leaders like Rick are seeking to out ahead of. You want to make yourself the person who receives that telegram, metaphorically speaking, and then you want to do better than your historical counterparts did—you want to take the right action. But getting people to tell you bad news is a fine art. Rick explains how he sets a tone of psychological safety to get the right information:

> *You definitely want to index with the right level of energy, but it can't be fly off the handle, scare people type energy. It's got to be the kind of energy that's appropriate for the situation. Also, I'm going to respond towards the issue, not towards that individual or not towards any people who may have created the problem or the chaos. And I'm going to thank them for bringing it.*

It takes a lot of equanimity to thank someone who's bringing you news that's going to be incredibly challenging to handle. But if the alternative is helplessly watching floodwaters rush over the hill, that moment of emotional control is well worth it.

Increase Your Personal Transparency Level to Treat People Like Adults, Driving Better Results

This strategy comes from a wonderful point Axialent partner Teryluz Andreu made in our interview. She noted that in a world where we are constantly asking people to work in more complex ways, we have to give them more information, and more context, to do so:

> *The right version of transparency is treating your employees as adults. Under legacy authoritarian or top-down ways of working, we treat people as kids who cannot behave. The paradox is that we ask them to do adult things, but then we treat them as kids. In contrast, leaders who are very*

Effectiveness Through Harnessing Transparency

<blockquote>

effective at all levels are the people who treat their employees as responsible, caring and engaged adults . . . and people live up to that bar.

</blockquote>

This is a terrific framing of how we need to reset the "give to get" dynamic. If we want people to work across teams, functions, divisions, departments, traditional silos, and so on, we need to give them more of the underlying story about why that work is happening. So many stoppages and misunderstandings result from people just missing pieces of information about each others' work—even in environments where it seems everything is known.

Be a Sense-Maker and a Myth-Buster

In addition to being the guy you bring bad news to, former Clorox CSCO Rick McDonald also strives to be the guy who sets the record straight, even when it's awkward to do so:

<blockquote>

I found in my last few roles I would spend some portion of my time debunking myths. That's why it's important as a leader to have a track record of staring at things objectively, pragmatically, not putting their own top spin on it when there's a true fact base, not minimizing something that was really damaging or went wrong and just saying, "Hey, we screwed up."

</blockquote>

In a world where a lot of information flies around all the time, if you can be the person who helps folks get their facts right, there's terrific trust-building upside even if the conversations are awkward at the time. We want to hear from people who are honest with us—and in hyper-transparent environments we're given more and more opportunities to be that person.

Once you've busted a few myths, there's another opportunity in hyper-transparent environments to be more effective and ultimately more influential, too: being the person who makes sense of all that disparate, confusing information. Leadership and organizational development leader Laura Fisher explains what that skill looks like:

> *There's a lot of focus on how do we frame to help people understand in the sentiment that the message is being sent, and things not being flipped and skewed. Information can be very fragmented. When we're sending a message, we have all of the unstated context and we know what's driving it. We know what we're trying to accomplish with it. We have all of this additional context. But people often take things in a different light or from a different perspective than it was intended. So good leaders help people understand the context in which a decision is made . . . which can be really hard when you have things that we can't share.*

The idea of giving people context for what's going on—even as rumors fly and conflicting data abounds—was another meta-theme of the interviews I conducted for this book. Almost everyone I talked to brought it up in some way. Accordingly, it's a great use of time to take a few extra minutes and help people around you understand the "why"—whether you're a CEO, at the front lines, or anywhere in between. We're all grappling with the fragmented information Laura alludes to—and context can be like water in the desert. It is a tough balance to do this fast enough to

Effectiveness Through Harnessing Transparency

have an impact—but with enough of a pause to do it thoughtfully—as culture and change management expert and Axialent partner Teryluz Andreu explains:

> *People are going to learn about what's going on anyway, so you need to be quick in your communications. However, there needs to be a center of consciousness in which people pause and say, why am I communicating this? What's really my intention in doing this or sharing this information? This is the step that sometimes doesn't happen.*

The ultimate level of sense-making, of course, is to make the actual actions behind the information make sense, and that's a lot harder. In our respective discussions, both Mercer partner Tauseef Rahman and Chief Human Resources Officer and professor Courtney Chisholm kept using a word that really sparked my imagination: coherence. It struck me that they both used the same word and both had a good deal of passion behind it. In his work with organizations, Tauseef sees increased transparency (starting with pay, but quickly broadening into all kinds of conversations around jobs and work), highlighting where the organization has actually made *incoherent decisions*. Behind the scenes, they don't have a consistent point of view on topics like what it means to be a high performer or how different geographies should be compensated relative to cost of living vs. cost of labor. Courtney coaches executives on the interaction between clarity and coherence—see the world clearly, communicate clearly, and your decision-making will have an underlying logic to it: coherence. This logic is critical to good leadership, especially under transparent conditions. Transparency makes leaders or organizations look weird because things actually are weird; they're not seeking to be unfair or random, but their decision-making is actually unfair and random. Coherence is the antidote.

Tauseef gives the funny analogy of asking someone if their house is clean. Most of us would say yes, sure it is . . . and then panic if the person asking was in fact at the door, ready to come up. We'd scurry around frantically wiping countertops and closing closet doors. Hyper-transparency means a constant stream of uninterrupted visitors; we're challenged to actually keep our (organizational) homes in shape! So, it's worth thinking about the ways you can personally do that—understanding that you may only be in charge of, let's say, a single closet shelf.

As Chapter 8 Comes to a Close . . .

Now that we've taken a clear-eyed look at hyper-transparency in the workplace, here are some strategies to consider.

For everyone

- *Operate in a transparency-friendly manner—emphasizing simplicity and clarity.* Coming back to Tauseef Rahman's clean-house metaphor, consider two houses. One is decorated in a very minimalist fashion, and the owners just don't have a lot of stuff. The other is decorated beautifully but elaborately, featuring a vast array of objects. Which is easier to keep clean for a bunch of unanticipated visitors? The first one, right? In a hyper-transparent world, it's the same with your working life. A more simple, minimalist, clear approach holds up better to constant and often unexpected or even unwanted scrutiny. Think about what you can simplify or even jettison to make what you do more explainable—it will save you countless cycles of parsing out complexity for folks not necessarily equipped to understand it.

Effectiveness Through Harnessing Transparency

If you're the boss

- *Set clear and—yes—transparent—"rules of the road" for transparency within your team.* Not everyone starts with the same definition of transparency, as consulting leader and private equity executive Michelle Stuntz explains:

You can put a dozen people in a room and say, "What does transparency in the workplace mean to you?" And you are going to get 12 different answers. And if you ask them all again, you might get another set of 12 answers. Really defining it for your team or your organization is important because people have different ideas in their head.

Take a step back and consider how you want information to circulate within your team. What level of explanation is needed? What channels should people be using? How often do different individuals and groups need to communicate with each other? What should be freely available information and what is legitimately "need to know" basis? Then, make those "rules of the road" clear to the team—including exceptions. For example, you may in general be pretty open about business strategy with the group—except when a highly confidential acquisition is in play. Being upfront about what you're not going to talk about before the situation is live can save a lot of hurt feelings and misperceptions on the back end.

If you're the big boss

- *Drive a transparency-friendly organization by being as coherent in core decisions as possible.* As complexity rises even for the smallest organization—and certainly for bigger ones—it's unbelievably easy to be a little all over the map. Many decisions are

Effective

made every day, often by disparate groups of people—leading to the lack of coherence that we heard about from Tauseef Rahman and Courtney Chisholm earlier in this chapter. Organizational consultant and Korn Ferry partner Maria Amato explains how this plays out across one very important dimension:

One vivid example is that you can't today have a huge disconnect between the promises that you're making to candidates and the reality that employees are experiencing. The number one source of information for candidates is almost always current employees and former employees. They're easy to find through people's networks and their opinions are readily available on social media.

If you're in a position to meaningfully guide your organization, in a hyper-transparent world one of the best things you can do is ensure that things basically line up behind the scenes. No organization is today in full control of what information will be discovered and shared among internal and external audiences alike, but if you operate in a way that is basically consistent and makes sense, no "reveal" should be too terrible.

In the last few chapters, we've described a few game-changing factors potentially impacting your effectiveness: work intensification, excess emotion at work, and hyper-transparency. And those often add up to one thing: chaos.

Work today can be incredibly chaotic. So, in Chapter 9, let's talk about what to do.

Effectiveness Through Harnessing Transparency

Chapter 9

Effectiveness Through Wrestling Down Chaos

When I sat down to write this chapter, I had to remind myself that chaos is not necessarily a bad thing. A blog post from the Fractal Foundation[1] actually put it quite beautifully: "Chaos is the science of surprises." The science of surprises? Two things I love: science, and surprises! In all seriousness, this blog (which is short, and gorgeously written, and I recommend reading in its entirety) makes a really good case for chaos as a useful framework for understanding life:

Chaos . . . teaches us to expect the unexpected . . . Chaos Theory deals with nonlinear things that are effectively impossible to predict or control, like turbulence, weather, the stock market, our brain states, and so on. Recognizing the chaotic, fractal nature of our world can give us new insight, power, and wisdom.

There's so much brilliance in that quote. Believing in a fully orderly universe is a recipe for a constant series of bad shocks; being at peace with the fact that you cannot control everything is, rightly, a foundational belief for everything from Buddhism to Alcoholics Anonymous.

Indeed, any Zen I've found in my own life has been the byproduct of not needing to make every decision, have every aspect of every situation nailed down, or always know what's coming. I truly believe there's a beauty in the chaos of the world—I wouldn't be on my 24th year of living in New York City if I didn't feel that way!

And yet—at work—I frigging hate chaos.

It sends my blood pressure soaring. What do you mean you don't have an agenda for this meeting? What do you mean the process just changed again and no one was told? What do you mean I'm in the already-insanely-complicated transfer pricing approvals system under my dead father's name? (That last one is a true story and my late father, who hated bureaucracy in only the way a dedicated scientist could, would have found the whole thing very funny.)

It turns out there's a useful distinction to be made here. There's the *natural chaos* of the universe, which is neither good nor bad: it just is. Then, there's *operating chaotically*. Which is BAD BAD VERY BAD DON'T DO IT . . .

Sorry, I triggered myself again.

So, we're going to split this chapter in two.

First, we'll talk about effectiveness amidst *natural chaos*—anything from a kooky customer to a sudden snowstorm to an unexpected technology development that sends your business strategy scrambling. For this set of strategies, imagine a surfer (again, not Ken—his job is just beach!) riding a series of waves. The waves change and come and go unpredictably, but the surfer balances upright.

Second, we'll talk about effectiveness when *things are operating chaotically*. Sorry, but this one is going to feel more like the scene in the zombie movie where the protagonists are trapped in a cabin, frantically shoving zombie arms away as the undead creatures reach in the window. Keeping this kind of chaos at bay is harder, but absolutely worth it (much like avoiding being bitten by a zombie, which has all kinds of upside).

Effective

Natural Chaos and the Effectiveness Architecture

We had prepared so well for a client workshop. We'd conducted thoughtful psychological assessments with an array of leaders; synthesized the resulting data artfully; prepared lively, intriguing exercises to engage the group; and teed up a fabulous executive from the client side to give the opening remarks.

And then we saw the weather forecast.

Wherever you live, there's some weather thing that bedevils you. Monsoons, sand tornados, those West Coast fires we talked about in Chapter 1 . . . and in the Northeastern United States, of course, it's snowstorms.

A monster one was headed our way—and it was coming the day of our long-planned workshop. While my colleagues and I were still squinting at the National Weather Service alerts, a call came in from our client, a world-famous consumer packaged goods company.

> *We have a protocol for snowstorms, and so we need to conduct this workshop early, so everyone can travel home safely well ahead of the weather. Can you be ready the day after tomorrow?*

Now, my partner in crime on this workshop was my former colleague, now founder and CEO of Perissos Partners, assessment and development guru John Pike. In addition to being absolutely brilliant at assessment and development, John has so much energy, he makes me look like I'm sleepwalking. So, the two of us being wired the way we are, our client got the most enthusiastic "HELL YES!" possible.

Despite the mad rush, it turned out to be one of my favorite workshops ever. Because they had such specific policies in place about what to do in case of wild weather, the client effortlessly

Effectiveness Through Wrestling Down Chaos

pivoted on all the logistics; all we had to do was show up in front of the room on a Sunday instead of a Wednesday and do our thing. Then we skedaddled back to our respective homes and hunkered down for what did turn out to be an impressive snowstorm.

In the ensuing months, I ended up telling the story to a lot of folks. The snowstorm protocol was cool and impressive: the client didn't hesitate for a second, they knew just what to do and whipped into action.

They had Methods. Good ones. (Just like the 9/11 doctors in Chapter 5!)

Methods are in fact the most powerful part of your Effectiveness Architecture in dealing with naturally occurring chaos. Strong, well-codified Methods are, after all, how the folks in Chapter 5 who do high-stakes jobs hold the chaos of the world at bay. By the time things get really chaotic, you don't want to have to sit there and figure out what to do. Remembering Dustin Liu's comment in Chapter 2 about how designers "know where to start again," when the chaos hits, strong Methods equals a bunch of good things to try.

While strong Methods are the slam dunk in fighting natural chaos, the People piece of your Effectiveness Architecture comes in handy too. Think back to our discussion of customer service and its technology travails. If something has gone wrong in a predictable way, you can often sort out your issue by talking to the chatbot or moving through the pre-coded menu options. "Press 1 to hear your monthly bill." Yeah, I can do that! Easy-peasy. But when things get chaotic, that's when you're sitting there going "Speak to a human. Speak to a human. SPEAK. To a HUMAN!" Chaotic situations get fixed in partnership with people.

Knowledge and naturally occurring chaos have an interesting relationship. Each interaction with the natural version of chaos both challenges your Knowledge and then builds it. When you pull the lens back and get Zen about the whole thing, natural chaos is

Effective

actually the fastest Knowledge builder possible, quickly showing you all the stuff you *don't* know so you can fix it. It just doesn't feel great at the time! Cloudflare Chief Cyber Solutions Officer Ramy Houssaini has a terrific perspective on this: "The leaders who thrive are those who treat chaos not as disruption, but as raw material to sharpen decision quality."

Similar to being strong in working with People, if your strength is Technology, you're often well equipped to combat natural chaos. My favorite story in this regard is the tale of Garrett Morgan, the man who perfected the stoplight.[2] Note that I didn't say *invented* the stoplight—that honor goes to John Peake Knight in 1868. Knight came up with the fundamental framing for stoplights, first for trains and then cars: a semaphore with a red light to tell you to stop and a green one to tell you to go.[3]

Knight's invention worked great for trains and okay for cars . . . until there were a lot of cars on the road. Suddenly, car accidents were everywhere. It was chaotic to the point of constant danger: the accident rate per 10,000 cars in 1913 was an astonishing *22 times* the 2023 rate.[4]

Enter Garrett Morgan, a successful serial inventor and the son of freed slaves. Morgan, who is also credited with inventing the predecessor to the World War I gas mask, had a simple but powerful epiphany: red and green weren't enough. There was a moment in between full-go and full-stop during which cars were crashing into each other—but there was no signal for that moment.

So, Morgan invented the yellow light—the piece of technology that really makes stoplights work.[5] He received a patent for it in 1923 and we are still using it more than 100 years, and countless saved lives, later.

Morgan's invention is a wonderful example of leveraging strength in Technology to bring the natural chaos of the world to heel. It's a classic story in many ways because technology is both

Effectiveness Through Wrestling Down Chaos

a contributing factor to the chaotic problem to be solved and ultimately integral to solving that problem. What made Morgan particularly effective in this instance is that he didn't display blind faith in technology—rather, he went looking for its blind spots and fixed them. He displayed what Tom Peck described in Chapter 4 as next-level technology skills around orchestration: understanding and solving for the complex relationship between early automobiles, traffic signals, and human beings. Flipkart president and board advisor Vipin Gupta explains the virtue of building technology without rose-colored glasses on:

> *For both data and systems, the guiding principle is to not design for a utopian world where everything looks and behaves the same. Instead, design for diversity from the start—that's how you stay future-ready for the next wave of change.*

Having reflected on how naturally occurring chaos both challenges and builds our effectiveness, let's get into some strategies. In an ever-more-naturally-chaotic working world, what are some strategies to turn the tide?

Scenario Plan, Then Iterate with Discipline

If chaos is the science of surprises, think of this as the strategy for surprise minimization. It's a mash-up of Knowledge and Methods. First, leverage your Knowledge of what could be happening/what could be about to happen to develop some quick scenarios. Then, leverage your arsenal of Methods. What are some battle-tested approaches you could *try* based on what scenario might be playing out? I'm emphasizing "try" there because that's the name of the game in chaotic times—trying, recording results, and trying again.

Effective

We generally intuitively understand this to be the right way to operate when things get chaotic, but don't make time to stop and do it—an ultimately more time-consuming approach on the back end when approaches fail and we have to go back and try something new anyway. Ferrovial Chief Information and Innovation Officer Dimitris Bountolos uses a lovely metaphor from the natural world to explain how the team he leads use this approach to make sure the most critical activities aren't knocked out at chaotic moments:

> *We are continually replanning to, as in a beehive, protect the queen in a chaotic environment. The most important piece is to understand which are the activities that we need to protect.*

Determine Your Maximum Degrees of Freedom (Human and Technological)

In this strategy, we're mashing up the People and Technology pieces of the Effectiveness Architecture. The fundamental question here is: How much room do I have to solve the problem? What resources can I call upon? A very mechanistic view of the world is actually helpful here: your toolkit to solve for naturally occurring chaos boils down to people, technology, and money . . . and to again "be so for real here." In financially optimized organizations, often there's not a lot of money to solve for anything that wasn't in the budget 8 months ago.

So, it's people and technology you're calling upon—and if these aren't your Effectiveness Architecture strengths, definitely go grab someone who's strong in those areas to help you figure out the next step. As veteran CIO Tom Peck observes, sometimes at the front lines of chaos, technology can really help us. We don't even know it, and we may not even be considering a technological solution to our woes:

> *Real engagement with technology can't be top down forced on the employee base or the colleague base. It also needs to be incubated in a grassroots manner. Too often our organizations and our employees and colleagues don't know the art of the possible or don't know what the technology is capable of doing. So that's part of the challenge too—education.*

Be Quick to Notice When the "Normal" Level of Chaos Has Escalated

Back to the opening of this chapter: there's a certain amount of natural chaos in the world. And as HR executive and organizational consultant Thiago Licias de Oliveira explains, "You can't fully keep chaos at bay—chaos is life at its most energetic. But you can learn to work with its rhythm." It's a beautiful thing to work adaptively with natural chaos. But under that same rubric, there's then a real value in identifying when you're *not* dealing with natural chaos . . . because your strategies will pivot.

For example, many businesses have a cyclical "busy season" that falls at the same time every year. That may be to do with corporate accounting, or winter holidays, but it's always a bit chaotic, and that's generally okay. Understanding, though, that the chaos seems a bit more chaotic this year, and finding the reason why, can save a lot of heartache and cycles. Has a seemingly small regulatory change thrown the whole system off balance? Has a supplier changed their business practices in a way that's throwing off your deliveries to customers? Don't be a "boiled frog"—the water might have actually gotten warmer, and calling out a time of abnormally chaotic chaos is absolutely worth it.

Effective

Operating Chaotically

Let's turn now from *natural chaos*—in which a butterfly flaps its wings in Argentina and causes a volcano to erupt in Hawaii—to *operating chaotically*—where Brad from Accounting just can't write a proper email and is driving you up the wall. This is the unglamorous, avoidable-but-pervasive kind of chaos.

I started my research on this subject with a couple of questions I ask myself a lot: Is work today operating more chaotically? And if it is, why?

Consensus across business literature: yes, and for some very normal reasons.

Start digging into chaos at work, and you'll find a million references to scale and complexity. Complexity, in particular, is seen as such a driver of chaos that you see the two being almost equated, in articles with titles like "Chaos In The House: Managing Workplace Complexity."[6] This all makes good sense. Larger groups of people are harder to organize, and once you've set something up in a complex fashion, you have definitely multiplied the ways it can go wrong.

And the facts are clear that more of us—at least in the United States—work for larger, more complex organizations than we did just a few decades ago. According to Bureau of Labor Statistics data,[7] roughly half of us (51%) work for companies with fewer than 500 employees. The other half (49%) work for companies with 500 employees or more.

This wasn't always the case: 30 years ago, smaller companies formed a much larger part of the landscape, representing 58% of the workforce. What caused this shift? Well, back then, the very largest companies were smaller. Walmart, which today has over 2 million employees,[8] then had a mere 500,000. Home Depot's workforce was about 50,000 folks strong—one-eighth of today's 400,000.[9] Most strikingly, Amazon, which today employs more than 1.5 million folks, was then a small start-up—fewer than 10 people, and still headquartered in Jeff Bezos's garage.[10] Contrast this explosive growth to the much slower growth of the actual US population (about 28% over the same period)[11] and you can see how larger organizations gained ground on smaller ones as common employers.

Okay, fine, you might say—but does size and complexity HAVE to equal chaos? The three companies in the last paragraph certainly do a lot, often quite effectively, to minimize chaos. It's not like they don't understand their own scale; on the contrary, what enables them to manage vast workforces is a lot of central organizing thinking.

But taking any particular company out of the equation, on a very basic level, greater complexity and scale quickly outstrips our brain's ability to manage it, which is where the chaos comes from. Researchers in Germany have neatly nailed some of the path that takes us from mere complexity to damaging chaos.[12]

They talk about the "NES" classification of systems:

- *N = natural systems.* This is the stuff nature cooks up brilliantly— all those wonderful real-world ecosystems that just run without interference or seeming thought. Imagine how a cleansing shower deep in the rainforest enriches the soil then evaporates back up into the ether to feed the next cloudburst. Elegant and wholly natural.

- *E = engineered systems.* These are systems humans think up and run successfully. The National Resident Matching Program (NRMP) is a fascinating example of an engineered system. The program, which has at its core a sophisticated algorithm, matches graduating medical students to fellowships and residency programs. NRMP manages to consistently place more than 90% of soon-to-be grads.[13] Not bad! While the system is constantly being improved upon, it's a good example of an engineered system because it took a highly chaotic, stressful

Effective

process of medical students basically begging their way into internships and created a relatively orderly and fair system instead.[14]

- *S = slipped systems.* These are systems humans set up which then broke! Slipped systems "do not adhere to cognition limits"—which is a very polite academic formulation of "our brains can't handle them" or even "they make no dang sense."

Using simple heuristics, like the human ability to only think about roughly seven things at a time, the researchers noted how often organizations are slipped systems. Think about how many C-suites have more than seven members (many of them!), or how many companies have more than seven organizing units (many of them!), or how many companies have more than seven initiatives (many of them!). We're setting up organizations that we struggle to then operate. And what happens? The research provides a neat list:

- "Tasks are not well defined" (*no one knows what to do*).

- "Roles and responsibilities are not well defined" (*no one knows who's doing what*).

- "No clear understanding by customers" (*perhaps worst of all—people can't figure out how to buy things from you*).

A more complex world of work—often operating at a greater scale—means that we're more likely to be operating in a slipped system—where jobs are muddy, responsibilities unclear . . . and customers confused! It's not that we want to operate more chaotically in the current moment, it's just that conditions are such that it's more likely to happen. So, let's talk about how organizations, teams, or people that *operate chaotically* (including you, yourself operating chaotically!) can impact your personal Effectiveness Architecture.

173

Operating Chaotically and Your Effectiveness Architecture

As someone for whom Knowledge is my core strength, I used to get incredibly frustrated by chaotic work situations that caused my Knowledge to hit its limits. After all, I know so much! This particular situation is only challenging because it's so deeply stupid! What ended up helping me was making a mental file entitled something like "Stupid Crap That's Happened at Work and What to Do About It."

I visualized sticking in this imaginary file folder standard operating procedures for every dumb thing that's ever happened in my vicinity (sometimes because of me, sadly). The time someone accidentally shared their screen with a chat about the client during a big pitch? The time I mistakenly insulted the work the client was most proud of? The time the absolute wrong person got added to the meeting? The (many) times we sent the wrong deliverable? All these instances, and their painful associated learning about how to dig myself and my team out, went in my mental file. Cringey though the mental file is, it has helped me on so many occasions (and believe me, has fueled my own professional development!). There's a whole lot of effectiveness behind "This is unbelievably dumb, but the good news is I've seen it before."

If Methods is your core strength, folks operating chaotically around you poses an interesting challenge. On the one hand, you may react similarly to folks who are strong in Knowledge, from a slightly different perspective: "How can anyone work this way?" If your gift is systematically getting a disparate array of things done well, it's not exactly energizing to watch others do the exact same thing terribly. On the other hand, you're well positioned to help solve for chaotic operations. You just have a similar "Goldilocks issue" to folks who are strong in the People part of the Effectiveness Architecture and operating in highly emotional environments—you're challenged to pitch in and sort things out, but not too little (ultimately unhelpful) and not too much (helpful but personally draining).

Interestingly, having People as a core strength can actually be a superpower in environments where people are operating chaotically. Quite similarly to interacting with natural chaos, being strong at the informal part of work—the part that's negotiated person to person—really comes in handy when things are all over the map due to those same people. Aspirationally, you may even be able to influence your closest colleagues to operate less chaotically, teaming up with folks strong in Methods who can then showcase a different way of working.

Finally, if Technology is your strength within the Effectiveness Architecture, your closeness to electronic systems may prove quite useful when people are operating chaotically. If you can develop real facility around guiding people back to accurate data and proper analytics, that can damp down a certain amount of corporate swirl.

Chaotic Operations: One Key Thing to Watch Out For

Before we get into general tips on effectiveness in operational chaos, I want to share something my research turned up that genuinely alarmed me. After all, "knowing is half the battle" and this information will help make you more effective when folks are operating chaotically at work.

I'll quote directly from one key meta-study: "Analyses reveal that all forms of incivility except sexual harassment are rooted in organizational chaos."[15]

Wow, really? I had always taken chaotic ways of operating as just inherently crummy—inept, incompetent, annoying as heck—but not per se malignant. But this research, reflecting a review of a number of studies, is saying something far worse: similar to crimes occurring under the cover of darkness, chaos at work actually provides a cloak for terrible behavior: "supervisory bullying, worker–customer conflict and co-worker infighting."

That's not cool. And it adds a different dimension to how you should think about effectiveness in this sort of chaotic context. We always want to assume positive intent in any given interaction, but in environments where people are operating chaotically it is important to vet for uncivil behavior and the impact it's having. Here are a few good questions to ask yourself in this context, based on these research findings:

- *Is anyone—particularly at leadership level—using "chaos as a strategy" to justify bullying behavior?* The meta-study identified the relationship between chaos and bullying as more prominent than others: "The largest standardized effect of any relationship modelled is that of chaos on supervisory bullying."[16] To understand how this works, recall how Zeynep Ton's work pairs up standardization and empowerment.[17] When things run in a fairly orderly way, each individual employee has greater opportunity to learn, stretch, be creative, and innovate. It's also easier to meet your leaders' expectations and be seen as a high performer. Sadly, though, there are leaders who behave chaotically as a Trojan horse for bullying behaviors. When targets and objectives change constantly, suddenly no one's doing anything right . . . opening the door for anger and authoritarianism. It's important to keep an eye out for this particularly toxic combination of behaviors—and then to address it by working to dampen both the chaos *and* the bullying.

- *Could we have less conflict with customers if we operated less chaotically?* The answer is yes. Coming back to Tauseef Rahman and Courtney Chisholm's thinking in Chapter 8 on the importance of coherence—of all the pieces of the puzzle fitting together properly—customers often get angered by what they see as

Effective

incoherent behavior on the part of the organizations they deal with. "You said your top corporate value is reliability, but you can't send a technician out for 2 whole weeks?" Visible disconnects can set people off, leading to interactions that are time-consumingly bad for productivity and negative for worker health alike. To the extent that you can smooth pieces of operational chaos, you can mitigate the toxic impact of angry customers.

- *Are teams bickering with each other simply because everyone's working a bit chaotically?* The meta-study contains a compelling description of how this happens: "Chaos increases the likelihood that workers will interfere with one another as they struggle to complete their own work."[18] Who among us has not been one of the figures in that description at some point or another—either interfering with someone trying to get work done, or being interfered with? We tend to think team conflict is a function of clashing personalities, but when teams go to war with each other, it's thus critical to look at whether chaos itself is a driving factor. It may be that the array of personalities in the team is just fine (or even ultimately helpful to the cause), but that no one could keep from fighting at that chaos level.

Remembering that not all chaotic operations are tinged with malfeasance, being alert to the ways negative human interactions can manifest in chaotic environments can help preserve our effectiveness—but also our sanity.

Effectiveness When People Are Operating Chaotically

More broadly, what are our strategies for effectiveness when people are operating chaotically around us? There are definitely some moves to combat what can feel like an incredibly frustrating problem.

Define Your "Eye of the Storm"

When people are operating chaotically in complex and interdependent workplaces, it's easy to feel strangely vulnerable. The physics of corporate life is such that it requires incredible focus and energy to keep complicated work on track, but it seems to take a mere touch to knock it clean off the rails. One random question at the end of a meeting, one confused email from someone who wasn't on the original chain, or, worst of all, one chaotically wired leader shows up in town . . . and suddenly everyone's hard work is gyrating through the spin cycle. It's impossible to fully avoid this phenomenon, but you can establish "circles of protection" where you can, yourself, control the chaos level. Let's say your organization's performance management process runs chaotically. (No, I don't have cameras inside your organization! It was a good guess. This is a pain point for a lot of companies.) You probably don't have full control over that process, but you can control how you craft the ratings and write-ups for your team—making them simple, concise, and fact driven. It won't fully bake the chaos out, but it can make your and your team's experience of the process incrementally less chaotic.

Managing expectations can be a powerful weapon in the chaos battle here—if it's about what you can control, define that sharply and run a tight ship there. As Sysco CIO Tom Peck puts it, especially in "high operating tempo environments" (which is so many of us these days), "you need to manage the expectations of your boss, of your stakeholders, of your constituents, of your team, of your family, of your kids, of your spouse, of your dog." That last one made me think—I suspect I have managed the expectations of my dog poorly, and that's why I've ended up giving her a treat every single time I open the laundry closet.

Effective

Get Your Hands on Some Redundancy

In an over-optimized world, as former Clorox CSCO Rick McDonald explains, your bulwark against chaos is having a little wiggle room: redundancy in systems, redundancy in manufacturing operations, extra inventory, those things that are actually going to help you withstand whatever bit of chaos is going to come your way. It's like when you go to the airport: unpredictable events are predictably going to take place, but if you get there a few hours before your flight, at least you're not going to miss your plane as a result.

Now, don't get me wrong here: similar to trying to work more independently, trying to incorporate more redundancy and more cushion into how you operate can be a seriously counter-cultural move in many organizations. The key, then, is getting creative in creating pockets of redundancy. For example, are there members of other teams that work so closely with your team that you could, at a pinch, pull them in to help out at a chaotic moment? (This actually tends to be enjoyable and career building for the folks in question; a rare true win–win.) Do you have access to systems or budgets that are not core to your day-to-day work, but could be pulled in for a specific need? Being a bit scrappy can really pay off at pressured moments.

Know Your "Order and Chaos Muppets" and Deploy Each Accordingly

Few pieces of writing have shaped my worldview as completely as Dalia Lithwick's 2012 *Slate* piece, "Chaos Theory: A Unified Theory of Muppet Types."[19] With breathtaking clarity, Lithwick asserts that all people—like all Muppets—have a preference for either order or chaos. In Lithwick's view, Chaos Muppets include Cookie Monster, Ernie, Grover, Gonzo, Dr. Bunsen Honeydew, and Animal; Order

Muppets include Bert, Scooter, Sam the Eagle, and of course Kermit the Frog. Both groups need each other to build a healthy and balanced society.

No one wants a world of Cookie Monsters, shrieking and chewing up everything in sight, but no one wants a world of Kermit the Frogs either, who just think so much about every darn thing. So, you yourself are either an Order or a Chaos Muppet, and the folks around you at work belong to one camp or the other as well. Understanding who's who—and the value each group brings—can help you tap the right folks for the right help at the right time. Need more energy for a project? Call a Chaos Muppet. Need more structure? Call an Order Muppet. And so on.

Barricade Your Boundaries—and Think Strategically About Your Calendar—To Ensure You Make It to Fight Another Day

Over the years, I've heard the same insight from colleagues and clients alike, over and over: "You know what would get me a better work-and-life integration? Less chaos at work." For many of us, what snarls our ability to balance obligations to our employer with obligations to our family and, indeed, our own health is not normal-course-of-business activities. It's constant crises.

You know the feeling: you're about to head out to pick up your kid from after-school soccer practice and that audio signaling an incoming Teams call starts going. You feel a cold pain in the pit of your stomach: another 6pm mess is going to screw up kiddie pick-up and family dinner. AGAIN. This phenomenon is impossible to fully address (especially where operations across time zones means your family dinner is someone else's morning meeting), but in many cases you can take steps to box operational chaos into working hours . . . saving your sanity to fight the next crisis. For example, if a recurring meeting always seems to surface crisis information, hold it as close to the beginning of the day and the beginning of the week as you can—giving everyone maximum working-day and work-week time to solve. It can also be helpful to declare "no-fly" zones in the morning as kids go to school and in the evening around dinner/homework, and be responsive and helpful before and after those times.

As Chapter 9 Comes to a Close . . .

We've looked at two kinds of chaos in this chapter: natural chaos and operating chaotically. Knowing which is happening when will meaningfully help you be more effective as you battle whichever chaos type you're dealing with. But for any time when you're not quite sure—or, as often happens, both chaos types are happening at once—let's look at some approaches for any chaotic moment. Here are some strategies to consider:

For everyone

- *As per some amazing advice from Dr. Rebecca Parker, learn to be good at being interrupted.* Constant interruptions are a fact of life in today's chaotic workplaces. One study from UC Irvine showed that office workers spend just under 13 minutes on a task before getting interrupted; they then spend more than 25 minutes before they can get *back* to that task; and it's only after spending *another* 15 minutes on that task that they're back at the level of concentration they were at before they were interrupted.[20] Our concentration and attention take constant, damaging hits. Dr. Parker has, over the years, developed a great strategy to combat the impact of interruptions. When she sits down to do a task—say, writing notes about a patient she just saw—she mentally maps out the natural stopping points. If someone interrupts her before she's hit a natural stopping point, she asks them to wait for a moment

Effectiveness Through Wrestling Down Chaos

until she's completed the task to that level. Once she's hit a place where it's "safe to stop"—where key information has been captured and a thought arc is finished—she can turn her full attention to the person asking for it. It's an imperfect science, as of course in an emergency room environment things come in that cannot wait, but on the whole it maximizes her ability to ensure each piece of her job is done well. We can all do a version of this—every task has natural places you can pause, and places where, if you were interrupted, you would seriously lose your train of thought. Understanding where you can stop and then gently asking folks to wait for a moment can turn a frantic day into a somewhat more focused one.

- *Know your own natural tolerance for chaos and plan accordingly*. Organizational consultant Birke Bakker puts it elegantly:

Definitely check yourself on your tolerance for chaos before you start thinking about solutions. If you have a low tolerance for chaos, then focus on how can you create structure for yourself on the parts you can influence. On the other side, if you have a high tolerance for chaos remember to manage yourself carefully. Just because you thrive in chaos doesn't mean your team will and you may need to provide more structure than you personally require or like.

Remembering Lithwick's foundational work on Order vs. Chaos Muppets,[21] it's okay to be one or the other, we all are, but knowing which side of the fence you sit on will help you work best with others in challenging moments. Specific to the case of people operating chaotically, Courtney Chisholm advises people to also know their own "threshold for pain—how much organizational dysfunction can you tolerate?" You may have a line where you wave a white flag—and we'll talk about this more in Chapter 10.

If you're the boss

- *Be vigilant for where chaos is allowing bad behavior to thrive, and actively look to solve it.* So many of the negative outgrowths of organizational chaos that we looked at in the meta-study referenced earlier in this chapter (bullying, customer conflict, and team conflict) are most readily detected at team level. If you lead a team of any size, you're the natural person to figure out they're happening . . . and to get people to reverse course. During chaotic moments, keep an eye on not just the "what" but the "how." Even if you're in maximal crisis mode, there's no excuse for bullying. Similarly, while a certain level of team conflict is healthy when things are messy, if the messiness is serially *driving* the team conflict, it's time to make structural changes, not just counsel individuals on their behavior.

If you're the big boss

- *Find some practical ways to shape a chaos-resistant organization.* As A. O. Scott notes in a (suitably chaotic) 2024 *New York Times* article, chaos may be the seminal challenge of our time.[22] To the extent that you can insulate your organization from chaos, all other business objectives are within closer reach. There's no one prescription for each organization, but you can brainstorm within the themes we've looked at in this chapter: reducing organizational complexity, creating pockets of redundant capacity where feasible, scenario planning around chaotic situations that seem to recur; and understanding how chaotically folks in key roles behave. Explicitly addressing the chaos

Effectiveness Through Wrestling Down Chaos

question at organizational level can be a breakthrough step from playing defense to playing offense (as my fabulous former boss Sandeep Bhatia would put it).

Whew. We've just looked at four different phenomena in the world of work that can challenge your effectiveness: work intensification, emotional workplaces, hyper-transparency, and just now . . . chaos. Hopefully you've thought a bunch about how the core of your Effectiveness Architecture is challenged by these forces . . . and how you can be maximally effective amidst them.

But you might have a nagging thought right now: "Melissa, we've just spent nine chapters on effectiveness. And to be honest, I'm not sure I *can* be effective in my current job. Is that possible—for effectiveness to not be possible?"

Absolutely. I'm not going to bamboozle you. While so much of your effectiveness is in your hands to address, and we've talked through a lot of ways to do that, there is a moment when you need to yell "STOP!" Your exact current role as it's framed *may not work*.

How do you know if that's the case? And what do you do then? That's what we'll talk about in Chapter 10.

Part III

An Effective Future

Chapter 10

What to Do (Next) When Effectiveness Is Not Possible

Harry and Eddie had high hopes for their hat store. They'd already run a successful canteen together, they had a great location for the shop, and they had tons of connections in the Kansas City hat-buying community.

What could go wrong? Cash poured in initially. Hats were selling like hotcakes. But then an economic downturn hit, and they were forced to close the store, a mere 3 years after opening it.[1]

Eddie rebounded fine—he became a successful traveling salesman.[2]

Harry (Truman) became the 33rd President of the United States.

It sounds trite, but it's worth reminding ourselves that a successful career doesn't mean every job works out. We may know this intellectually, but in the moment, in each role, we often place heartbreaking amounts of pressure on ourselves to succeed. And, in general, looking to ourselves first and what we can control is 100,000% the right move. Nobody's getting anywhere by serially declaring their job impossible.

But that said: your job might be impossible. Or at least impossible to be truly effective at.

So, in this chapter we're going to look at two key questions:

1. How can I tell if I am in a job where I cannot be effective?

2. If that's the case, how do I think through my next steps?

Let me set a quick guardrail on the second question: I am not going to advise anyone to run off and quit their job without a thoughtful examination of their financial situation. My parents didn't assiduously work their way out of poverty for their idiot daughter to go write a book advising folks to just go find their bliss, monthly bills be damned—that's not reality for 99% of the world.

As organizational consultant Maria Amato notes, "People work for money and I think we really underestimate that. While people are motivated by purpose and a sense of achievement, very few of us would be doing our jobs for charity." We'll explore a variety of ways out of a broken or misaligned job, but all within the context that we need money to live and we need jobs to have money. Losing sight of that would be unforgiveable. This chapter has to be fueled by realism.

And realism tells us that not every job is set up for success. Let's look at the ways that can happen.

It Just Can't Be Done: How to Tell If You Can't Be Effective in Your Job

There are several common reasons why a job is not set up for effectiveness—some having to do with the job itself, some having to do with the job's alignment with the organization, and some having to do with the job's alignment with the individual in it. Let's look at each category and how it might show up in practice.

The Job Is Poorly Designed In and Of Itself

I spoke to two talented organizational consultants (and cherished former co-workers)—Birke Bakker, founder and CEO of Brightside Consulting, and João Gonçalves, partner at Korn Ferry—and they gave me near-identical answers on the question of what a broken job looks like. If what you're held accountable for cannot be achieved

Effective

via the resources and decision rights you're given, your job is broken. In simple terms, if you're given a problem without the wherewithal to solve it, that's a job problem, not a personal performance issue.

In jobs with a high level of engagement with the physical world, this tends to be less of an issue. No one expects you to be a truck driver without a truck. When we look at service roles, things start to erode: how many teachers are sent in every year without the right amount of school supplies for their class?[3] By the time we get to knowledge work, and the more we move up executive ranks, these issues become scarily common. You're not given a team to action on the work that needs to be performed; you're expected to "mobilize aligned resources via influence." You're told to build the right team, but you don't own hire/fire decisions. And so on. Organizations burn millions of dollars each year by plopping high-priced talent into jobs that fail Job Design 101. So, it's absolutely worth looking at whether what seems to make your job challenging actually makes it impossible: a fundamental mismatch between expectations and what you're actually armed with to deliver.

How this often shows up in practice: You are denied the resources needed to accomplish the key objectives of your job. You're expected to mobilize a lot of folks, none of whom report to you. (Beware of repeated references to "leading through influence!") You go to make decisions that are make or break for what you're supposed to accomplish, and discover those are not your decisions, or that your decisions are serially overruled.

The Job Is At Odds with the Organization's Overall Intent or Culture

Organizational consultant and author Mary Cianni really illuminated this one for me: "In some cases, people are resisting what the organization is doing and you're the person who's the spearhead for unwanted actions or initiatives." Ouch, and yes! This is unfortunately another

What to Do (Next) When Effectiveness Is Not Possible

category of broken job: the organization hired someone to do what the organization does not actually want to do—and you're that person! It's a well-intentioned mistake and often excruciating to live through as the individual in that role. I once had a darkly funny conversation with another consulting leader where we ended up agreeing that one should not accept a role where the organization says they're seeking a "change agent"—because you're being hired to swim upstream in just this way.

There's even a version of this, organizational consultant João Gonçalves explains, where your job conflicts with the entire culture of the organization. He cites as an example organizations' frequent attempts to create "innovation in a box"—hiring whole teams of folks to innovate because the overall culture is so risk-averse that it stamps out any organic innovation that might occur. The new hires' innovation, of course, also gets stamped out—but they personally get blamed, or blame themselves, when in reality there was no chance of success.

If you're interviewing for a newly created role in an organization, it's worth asking what was the blocker to someone doing this work in the normal course of business for an existing job. You may end up hearing about dynamics that will impede the success of the new role as well. As consulting leader and private equity executive Michelle Stuntz explains:

> *There are things about an organization that no one's ever going to tell you but that are very very true and are more important to understand than what's written down in a handbook anywhere. They're not codified and they might not even be logical, but you also can't change them. Any time spent trying to change them is beating your head against a brick wall.*

Effective

How this often shows up in practice: People repeatedly tell you they do not understand, or are opposed to, the core intent of your job. Your job is explicitly framed to get people to do the opposite of what organizational incentives tell them to do (e.g., you're supposed to get salespeople to collaborate across territories, but those salespeople's bonuses depend only on sales in their own territories). You constantly feel like you're hitting organizational tripwires, with people becoming upset or agitated by your performing the normal activities of your role. You yourself have started to question what you're doing due to the sheer degree of day-to-day resistance.

Your Manager Prevents You from Being Effective

Note, this one is not framed as "your manager stinks." It's a sad fact of contemporary life—and many of the folks I interviewed brought this up—that a large proportion of leaders fall short on basics like communicating clearly, displaying appropriate empathy, or critically, organizing work such that it can be performed properly. Your boss may well stink—and that's often the reason why many people leave organizations, according to both classic and recent research.[4] They may engage in behaviors you find unpalatable or even detrimental to your mental health, and that's a hugely valid reason to make some sort of change. No argument there.

But they may also have skills gaps in quiet, less perceptible ways that meaningfully impede your effectiveness. For example, many otherwise kind and well-meaning leaders tread all over their teams' decision rights. They're not blatantly micromanaging, but they're not letting anyone else make decisions, either—thus impeding the effectiveness of everyone who works for them. As João Gonçalves describes it, your leader's behaviors can turn a well-designed job in theory into a poorly designed one in practice.

How this often shows up in practice: You have a "last-mile" problem, where initiatives proceed at pace until they get to your manager and then stop in their tracks. Your manager routinely seems to take things that should be attached to your role—resources or decisions. In the worst cases, your manager engages in bullying behaviors that leave you ruminating angrily or sadly, and thus unable to operate effectively.

The Organization Tolerates Underperformance

In our interview, organizational consultant Birke Bakker crystallized something that had been nagging at the edges of my brain for many years—it's ultimately impossible to do good work in an organization that's overly tolerant of bad work:

> *One thing that can quietly make people very ineffective is cultures where underperformance is tolerated. It might feel relaxed at first—especially for conflict-avoidant managers—but for the people that actually want to get things done (your high performers) it's incredibly frustrating. It's a silent killer of motivation if I work hard and do a great job, yet you slack off and we're rewarded the same.*

Birke's words really resonated. It's not actually relaxing to work somewhere with no standards—or worse, in a workplace that seems to *prefer* mediocre work. If you have any wiring at all to aspire to excellence—and if you're reading the tenth chapter of a book on effectiveness, it's a reasonable guess that you do—it's frustrating and tiring to be surrounded by folks who do not seem to know what good looks like.

How this often shows up in practice: Performance reviews seem disconnected from performance data, and rewards seem wholly disconnected from performance. People keep telling you to chill out, lower your standards, and stop being so intense. Mediocre performers are celebrated and often long-tenured.

The Job or Way the Organization Operates Is in Fundamental Conflict with Your Values

Sometimes the issue is all the way at the root—your values do not match those of the place you work, or the work you're asked to do. Head of the NYU Stern Initiative on Purpose and Flourishing, Suzy Welch's book *Becoming You* really brought this issue to life for me—providing a language of values that, frankly, explained some profound discomfort I've felt in my career. When I interviewed her, Suzy was pithy and clear on how insurmountable a values conflict is:

> *You need to know what your values are and whether or not they're aligned or misaligned with your organization's. And if they're misaligned, understand that they're not going to change their values. It's an organization. There's a lot of them and there's one of you. You have a right to yours and they have a right to theirs.*

It's critical to think about this particular state of the world with that level of stark lucidity. We often think we can "hide in plain sight," not quite seeing the world the same way the organization around us does, but eking it out every day anyway. But as Welch's research makes clear, we can't be effective when what we truly value is not what our workplace values. It's important to test for this periodically; organizations' values may drift over time, and you may end up out of alignment with an employer that once truly resonated for you.

How this shows up in practice: You can't shake the feeling that you at heart value different things than the people around you. Your job

What to Do (Next) When Effectiveness Is Not Possible

asks you to do things that seem to conflict with who you are as a human being. You feel as though no one at work understands you.

For Whatever Reason, You Can't Seem to Get Traction

Sometimes, the blockage isn't visible—but it's palpable. As Suzy Welch notes, it's critically important to be alert to cues that signal you're not getting anywhere—and to trust your gut as you do so:

> *The work will tell you. You can read the room: Are you progressing? Are you getting promoted? Are people making eye contact? Every 4 months or so, you should check-in with your boss and say, how's it going? But that said, it should be intuitive: do you know when you're in love? Same idea.*

Organizational consultant Mary Cianni heartily concurs, and talks through how she coaches leaders to get to that realization: "Nine times out of 10, the person knows that they're not doing well. And in part helping them to see, and to look at is a gift." Questions like: "There was this meeting and you weren't included. What was that about?" Or "You were trying to set up these meetings with leaders as part of your remit of what you needed to do, but you were getting roadblocked. What is that telling you?" You may even hear signals in your own body, as HR executive and organizational consultant Thiago Licias de Oliveira describes: "In my experience, the body knows before the mind does. You'll feel dissonance: energy drains, a sense of being out of place, chronic tension. But we often override those signals—until we break open."

How this shows up in practice: You are serially not recognized for your work, in formal and informal ways. You are excluded from key meetings, emails, or other places people gather that are integral to your work. You struggle to get time with the co-workers you need to partner with to accomplish your objectives.

Effective

Two caveats on this one:

1. First, what I described above could also be the experience of someone who is working at an organization that struggles with inclusion—nothing to do with traction in the role. If that's what's happening to you, please understand that no one is blaming you for your experience and do not gaslight yourself. Please take your gifts to an organization that appreciates them!

2. Second, in a world of increasingly limited organizational resources, it's critical to take into account a realistic picture of what rewards even look like. I've seen folks get incredibly frustrated about raises and promotions when . . . no one was getting a raise or a promotion. So, make sure you contextualize your view of your own progress to what's actually afoot at your organization. (And it's also a problem that no one's getting a raise or a promotion! Just a different problem.)

If what you're experiencing matches one of the above six scenarios (or often, more than one of the above six scenarios), it's time to start exploring what to do. Let's talk about what that looks like.

When You Can't Be Effective: Understanding Your Options and Taking Action

It's no small thing to admit you can't be effective in a particular role. For so many of us, this cues up some incredibly negative self-talk:

"I failed."

What to Do (Next) When Effectiveness Is Not Possible

I've been there personally, and I've worked with a number of executives going through this moment, too. Honestly, you have to take a second, mourn, and reflect. Something you thought would be amazing, wasn't. And there are doubtless lessons for you, both around how you choose your work and how you perform it.

But resist excessive self-flagellation. It's going to be impossible to take the right next action if you're obsessed with self-blame and stuck in a cycle of rumination. And the next right action really matters.

I can't tell you the exact right action for your circumstances—particularly given the economic caveat from earlier. I can tell you that, as multiple brilliant coaches I interviewed for this book told me, simply mentally testing out options and being curious about different paths will lighten your anxiety load and move you closer to the right place.

Let's look at some possible paths out of each of the six situations where you genuinely cannot be effective in your job.

If Job Design Is the Problem

Have a job-centric conversation with your manager. Let's say you're in a scenario where your job has a design problem—a mismatch between expectations and resources. Most of us approach this discussion from the point of view of "here's what I need to do this" or even "I don't think I can do it and here's why." Try a reframe instead: "This is what my job needs to be successful." Not you, your job. Move the conversation to a place of objectivity around job wiring, not a subjective discussion of how you personally utilize resources.

Evidence helps. Do others in similar roles have different resources or decision rights? Does the job "work" differently at other organizations? It may seem like silly extra work to create what amounts to a business case for the job you're already in, but if that added step

Effective

helps you stay with a manager and/or organization you love *and* be more effective at what you do, it's well worth it.

If the Job Is at Odds with the Organization's Intent or Culture

Make a clear call on whether you want to do something else at that organization, or if you want to work on that sort of intent somewhere else. Let's say you get appointed Chief AI Officer at a large regional bank seeking to expand fast. You get there, and folks are so allergic to AI that people physically drop off calls every time the initials L, L, M appear in order. There are two paths you can take. If you find working at a bank in hypergrowth mode interesting and energizing, you could get another technology job at the bank; if specifically leading an AI team is your dream, you could shop around for another Chief AI Officer role at a different organization. Either path is valid: it really depends whether you are energized by the journey of a particular role in an organization-agnostic way, or find yourself intrigued by an organization (above and beyond the current misalignment in your role).

If Your Manager Prevents You from Being Effective

Work your way through the concentric circles of opportunities that start with that manager but lead to the wider world. Imagine your current manager sitting in the bullseye of an archery target. Your conversations should start in that smallest central circle: at least try to raise the issue with your manager about how they are limiting your effectiveness. Be evidence-driven (specific on particular actions) and borrow some of the language from the job-design conversation above. It's not that they're tripping *you* up—it's that they're messing with the effectiveness of your *role*. Let me be clear: this may not work. But it's worth trying, especially if you feel your manager is well-intended and kind, but bumbling.

What to Do (Next) When Effectiveness Is Not Possible

The next circle-out would be to explore roles with different reporting lines in the immediate vicinity of your role. If you're truly energized by the underlying intent of what you're doing, but feel your manager can't get out of your way, exploring these roles with the appropriate discretion can be a great move. The next circle-out would be roles afield of your current work—which are worth looking into if you really like your organization and don't want to change companies. The final circles, of course, sit outside the organization: roles at similar companies, or outside the industry altogether. But it's worth working concentrically if there are elements of your current job and organization that really do work for you.

If Your Organization Is Too Tolerant of Underperformance

Pack a "go bag" (understanding a move might take a minute). In sharp contrast to the prior scenario, this is not a time to thoughtfully iterate. File a tolerance for underperformance under "gravity"—forces you can't fight (!)—and start looking elsewhere immediately, knowing a thoughtful switch can take time. Most 99% of the time, you are not going to single-handedly convince an entire company to do better—this kind of wholesale culture shift generally requires the signing-on of a good chunk of the C-suite and a lot of time to pivot. If you are at CEO or C-suite level and truly want to take this challenge on, we are all rooting for you. But for most of us, it's better to seek out a company full of like-minded individuals who see good work the same way we do.

If the Job or the Way the Organization Operates Is in Fundamental Conflict with Your Values

Take a minute, know yourself, then pivot. It's extraordinarily valid to make a change based on a values misalignment. Like the prior scenario, you're not going to change the whole organization . . . you will

Effective

need to, in some way and in some timing, vamoose. It's important, though, to know exactly what your values are before you make a leap—you could leave one job because it conflicted with a single value you hold and end up in another job that conflicts with another value. Make sure a full inventory of your values precedes action.

If You Just Can't Get Traction

Time to do some "tiny experiments." In our interview, Senior Associate Director of the NYU Stern Initiative on Purpose and Flourishing, Dustin Liu, talked about the value of micro-scale experimentation in helping the brain make life-changing pivots. He describes how just trying smaller different choices in a low-consequences way activates the brain to make larger changes: "Hey, how do you actually just test what it feels like to be a baker? How do you test what it feels like to start a different morning routine? I think those tiny experiments really add up."

It's the perfect methodology for this scenario, where you don't have perfect clarity on what's gone amiss—but you know something is wrong. You're making your mind free and limber—building space for new possibilities by taking the immense pressure off a single-point decision. In this scenario, it's helpful to consider the possibility that a mismatch can sometimes be a function of your talents vs. the company's lifecycle. Similar to a failed romantic relationship, you can have met a company at the wrong time in its life!

For example, as long-time search consultant and board advisory Mark Polansky notes, when he looked to place CIOs, their skill set had to align with:

> . . . the stage to which the company has progressed. Is the company already way ahead of the pack in technology and just need somebody to keep that going? Or is the company

What to Do (Next) When Effectiveness Is Not Possible

way behind and looking for a digital transformation, not a business transformation? Or are they at the stage of a business transformation?

Depending on the conditions on the ground, a very different person might fit. It's entirely possible to be at the right company at the wrong time.

Getting Back in Touch with Your Effectiveness During a Setback

Even while you're taking constructive steps to get yourself into a role where you can be effective—whatever that looks like—it's easy for negative self-talk to persist. You chased away the "I failed" idea by embarking on a thoughtful course of action, but at 3 am, the terrible thoughts creep back in. You start to wonder if you ever were good at what you do . . . or if you'll ever be successful again.

It's time to re-anchor yourself in what makes you effective—using evidence.

First, go back to some of the work you did in Chapters 3 and 4 around identifying where you're strong in the Effectiveness Architecture. If you took the self-assessment, have a look at those results.

Then, as if you're preparing for an interview, assemble some real-life proof points from your area of strength within the Effectiveness Architecture. If you're strong in Knowledge, it might be having created a valuable piece of intellectual property; if you're strong in Methods, it might be an operational turnaround; if you're strong in People, it might be bringing together a team across traditional silos; if you're strong in Technology, it might be using a new technology to drive high-return-on-investment innovation.

But then, daydream a bit. Thinking again about your area of core strength within the Effectiveness Architecture: What *else* might it

Effective

allow you to do? For many years, my strength in Knowledge allowed me to write articles and whitepapers; it was only relatively recently that I started imagining that that same strength could make me effective at writing books. I wish I'd had that conversation with myself sooner . . . but it's never too late.

Having an evidence-driven conversation with yourself about why you're effective—but also how that effectiveness can continue to grow and change—will both quiet the 3 am voices but also help you sell yourself better as you take on your next steps. Whether you're staying in the same job with some tweaks to resources or starting your own business in a completely different industry, re-anchoring in your effectiveness gives you a forward momentum that pushes you through change and disruption.

As Chapter 10 Comes to a Close . . .

Let's ponder some final strategies around that moment of realizing you're in a situation where effectiveness may not be possible.

For everyone

- *Think about your job like someone who studies work.* Organizational consultant João Gonçalves had a funny observation during our interview: people consultants have been talking about job descriptions going away for years, but they never seem to go anywhere! In his view—and I heartily agree—job descriptions persist because we need some fundamental "anchor" as to what we're meant to be doing. So, while it would be weird to sit there and read your job description every day, there's definitely some insight to be had by periodically examining the levers that make your job work (or not!) in the same way someone who studies work would. What is the core intent of your job, and does it still align with the organization's purpose

What to Do (Next) When Effectiveness Is Not Possible

and culture? Do the resources you're given match the account-abilities you're tasked with? Knowing whether the basics that fuel effectiveness are in place enables you to take fast action if something's misaligned.

If you're the boss

- *Scrupulously examine your own actions through the lens of the effectiveness of your team, again using a lens that takes into account what makes jobs work.* None of us want to be that manager who's short-circuiting the people who work for them, but many of us are at different times. Especially when the pressure is on us from leadership or the external environment, it's tempting to just hurdle over job design barricades right and left. Resist the urge! In the same way that folks should be looking at the basic alignment of their job with the organization's core work and the accountabilities of their job with the resources given to them to do it, as a manager you'll want to look at whether your behaviors disrupt any of that. For example, have you assigned someone on your team to a "pet project" of yours that conflicts deeply with the organization's overall intent? Without clear guardrails and protections, with excellent intentions you may be setting them up for failure. You need to be a bit of a crack job designer yourself, as leadership and organizational development leader Laura Fisher explains: "Leaders need to take that step back and say, is the job we're giving you actually realistic? And is the job that we're saying it is and the job that we're actually reinforcing on a day-to-day the same?"

If you're the big boss

- *Make sure you're creating foundational organizational conditions for effectiveness—including, most of all, capable managers.*

Effective

CHRO and Georgetown professor Courtney Chisholm states without reservation that the most transformative move organizations could make today would be to "give everyone a competent emotionally intelligent manager." In addition to capability around empathy and communication, competence includes the skills around getting work right from the tip above; every manager should be making sure their team's work is structured properly. As UVA professor Jim Detert notes:

What we ignore is that what people spend almost all their time actually doing is their job, not listening to leaders spout off, whether it's really inspiring or not. After they're done hearing you, they have to go back and do their job.

At organizational level, you want to make sure that you're bringing managers to the fore who are both able to truly connect with their teams (the "cool stuff" around emotional intelligence) and know their team's work well enough to manage it (the "boring stuff" around architecting work properly).

A moment when you realize you cannot be effective can be a dark one. But in Chapter 11 we'll turn our attention to the light at the end of the tunnel: the future of effectiveness, and what next-level effectiveness looks like.

The Future of Effectiveness

You know who feels effective right now? Me! I'm almost done with my second book.

All kidding aside, thanks for sticking with me through the journey. We've looked at how to think about your work with an analytical eye; how to dissect effectiveness into four essential pieces (Knowledge, Methods, People, and Technology); how to figure out where your strength lies within the Effectiveness Architecture; how to combat forces that challenge your effectiveness (work intensification, emotional workplaces, hyper-transparency, and chaos); and finally, what to do if it's becoming clear you cannot be effective in your current role as framed.

That's a lot of intellectual and emotional work. I hope you've come away with some concrete strategies to try and some provocation about issues in your working life. Like everything else worth doing in life, effectiveness is a daily grind, but if your working tomorrow is a little better than your working today, this book has done its job.

Before we end our journey together, though, I want to talk about the future of effectiveness.

There's an incredible amount of chatter in the environment right now about how useless humans are going to be going forward—how AI will straightforwardly automate most of the work we currently do, shrinking human workforces dramatically.

My reaction to this line of thinking is literally unprintable, so I'm going to let brilliant MIT AI researcher Isabella Loaiza weigh in instead on how believing in automation over augmentation represents a short-sighted folly:

> *We're human and often it is easier for us to see and understand things that are closer to us physically and temporally. Automation tends to happen to the activities that we do today. So we see that happening in real time, but the big chunk of augmentation is going to come in the future and that's harder for us to see because we're embedded in our everyday activities, right? Fortunately or unfortunately depending on how you want to see it, we are limited by our own imaginations . . . but we don't have to be. We can imagine a future where augmentation is the real promise of AI.*

There's an elegant truth in her statement: there is no human future of work other than what we collectively imagine. As I interviewed an array of smart folks from industry, academia, and consulting for this book, I was intrigued to see a pretty consistent vision of the future of effectiveness emerge. From a variety of vantage points, my interviewees universally characterized this view of what next-level effectiveness looks like as we hurtle into an uncertain future. Dots-connecting. Sense-making. Coherence. Systems thinking. Shaping and providing context.

What I heard over and over was that the most effective people of the next age put it all together and make it make sense. Master consultant Tauseef Rahman and CHRO Courtney Chisholm both separately, and passionately, opined on the value of coherence as a leadership and organizational principle. On the human front,

Mark Polansky offered a powerful description of bringing the right people together as a superpower (it's Mark's personal superpower, for sure):

> *Being a good people connector means understanding the question of which people will go with other people. Who will be able to communicate, not necessarily agree with everything, but not be frictional, be able to work together, and to share together. You must be able to judge character, too. I'm always looking at people and saying, who should know this person? Who would this person do well to know?*

Cloudflare Chief Cyber Solutions Officer Ramy Houssaini, like Tauseef Rahman, saw a power in uniting whole networks of humans too—thoughtfully with a win for everyone:

> *I see myself as a super-connector. Authentic interactions and trust are the foundation, but I always try to inject value into every relationship so there's no asymmetry. In the AI era, these human networks—rooted in reciprocity and purpose—will be the most powerful advantage any of us can have.*

CIO Dimitros Bountolos spoke about a whole group of emerging talent with the ability to look across traditional silos and put together a whole-organization vision:

> *There's an incredible opportunity here for those employees that understand the whole picture and have transversal, not superficial understanding—a coherent perspective of the map and all the pieces that we need to put in place in*

The Future of Effectiveness

*order to accomplish the overall goal. Inter-domain knowl-
edge is going to become much more critical, as well as
inter-sectoral or inter-departmental understanding.*

Flipkart president and board advisor Vipin Gupta sees start-up executives stepping out of their proscribed roles and deploying whole-organization thinking that we'd all do well to emulate:

*Most start-up executives naturally operate as "multilin-
gual," but that's not often the case in large corporations. If
you sit in a start-up executive team meeting, it's hard to tell
who's marketing, who's legal, who's finance, and who's
technology—the language blurs because they're all thinking like owners.*

CHRO Courtney Chisholm described how this kind of big picture understanding plays out at leadership level:

*The most effective leaders are able to zoom in and zoom
out. The zoom out has to do with being able to see how
things are interdependent, the designing of a role, the culture of the organization, the tools that you give to a person,
and the clarity in how decisions are made . . . then, they
can zoom back in to see how their contributions fit
within that.*

HR executive and organizational consultant Thiago Licias de Oliveira offers a different version of this leadership toggle between the big and small pictures: "Great leaders help others see the 'part–whole dance.' Sometimes we are the system. Sometimes we're part of it."

Effective

Context and story are huge. Organizational consultants Birke Bakker and João Gonçalves both discussed the ability to contextualize one's work to the greater ecosystem of work in the organization as a next-level skill that folks who design systems of work would advise us all to get better at. Leadership and organizational development leader Laura Fisher and Axialent partner Teryluz Andreu both spoke about the power of leaders who can contextualize fragmented information for their teams. Ramy Houssaini believes the most exciting technological progress will come from people who know how to incorporate context, noting that "the most gifted 'AI experts' of tomorrow will be domain experts—economists, biologists, financiers, and creators—who bring deep context and imagination to the table."

Indeed, integrating everything into one cohesive narrative matters a lot. CIO Tom Peck looks for storytelling as a key trait even for the most technical roles he interviews for. Professor and author Suzy Welch emphasizes how important it is for your story to make sense to you and your values (a piece that often gets lost in a world where we frantically massage our narratives to appeal to the outside world). Roland Rodriguez fretted about the folks who take videos of him and his firefighter co-workers as they eat lunch, as those folks capturing a tiny piece of the fire crew's day *don't* have the whole story.

The whole story matters.

There are a few things I love about this crowdsourced view of the future of effectiveness as synthesizing the world and making sense of it all.

First, you can participate in it no matter what your area of strength is within the Effectiveness Architecture. Knowledge folks can break down traditional barriers between disciplines to make us all smarter. Methods folks can help us better systematize work

The Future of Effectiveness

by connecting what seem to be disparate activities. Folks who excel in the People dimension can do what Tauseef, Mark, and Ramy do, and bring people together to learn from each other thoughtfully and consistently; folks who excel in the Technology dimension can contribute more of the (desperately needed) skill Tom Peck talked about in Chapter 4: orchestration between technologies for a better end result for users.

Second, while the ability of AI to detect and reproduce patterns continues to improve, humans remain vastly, vastly better at making sense of the world. For example, while writing this chapter I asked my word-processing program to generate a list of synonyms for "visionary." Simple right-click functionality, not even large language model territory. It gave me "unrealistic," "impracticable," "quixotic," "fanciful," and "unworkable." Not to be a weirdo English major here, but those five words, all of which have quite negative connotations, are not useful synonyms for "visionary," a word with highly positive connotations. Technology can reproduce some of the lyrics it hears, but it remains insensitive to the underlying music of the world. Humans can hear that music acutely.

The idea of shaping the story even as technology continues to advance is a hopeful one. In the EPOCH model of human capabilities in the AI age—of which AI researcher Isabella Loaiza is a co-author—the "H" stands for hope. Loaiza proudly notes that not only is hope her favorite part of the model, but it's also the one with the highest statistically significant regression coefficient in their big-data analysis of job tasks. In other words, hope is the most important working human skill in a world of galloping technology. Hope works: some of the best people I've worked with have been exceptionally good at bringing authentic positivity into the workplace. I'll quote Birke Bakker on this front: "Keep a very happy mind. Have some fun. Find the people that you vibe with.

Effective

Having a sense of humor in work has gotten me through the worst days."

So, I hope that this book has given you some hope. For me, the idea that we can all be amazing at the work we do is an energizing one. Go forth and be great, and please come back and tell me what worked and what didn't. I want to be more effective too!

We spend so much of our lives at work. If we all do what we do a bit better, we can change the world.

Great work is a great goal. Be effective.

The Future of Effectiveness

The Effectiveness Self-Assessment

The following is a short quiz to help you understand your strengths and challenges within the Effectiveness Architecture.

For each question, give yourself the following points:

1: I'm not good at this at all

2: I'm not great at this

3: I'm okay at this

4: I'm pretty good at this

5: I really excel at this

Once you've taken all sections, total up your scores and compare. Where do you see yourself as being stronger, and where do you see more challenges? There are no objectively "high" or "low" scores—only where you yourself perceive relatively more capability. Understanding this helps you better navigate the workplace (and honestly—the world!).

Knowledge

- I know what the basics are for someone to be good at my job.

- I feel like I have the basic understanding to be good at my job.

- I'm up to speed on the most recent developments in my field.

- When something comes up at work that I don't know, I know who or where to find the answer.

- I have ways to constantly learn about how to do my job better.

- Day to day, I know the data or facts I need to be effective in my work.

- Based on the information I have, I can make decent decisions at work.

- At work, other people come to me with questions.

- I don't waste a lot of time in each work day trying to figure information out.

- I understand both the theory of my job and the practice of how it should be done well.

Methods

- I have a good concept of how to structure each day to get things done at my job.

- I have strategies for when things go wrong, things change, or things become chaotic at work.

- I don't often have to rethink how to do core aspects of my work—I have a natural flow.

- I can easily explain how different parts of my job fit together.

- It would be straightforward for me to teach someone how to do my job.

- It's clear to me what I should prioritize within any given day at work.

Appendix: The Effectiveness Self-Assessment

- I'm rarely truly surprised at work.

- I know what's not part of my job.

- I can relate parts of my job to each other that someone might not see from the outside.

- If given the opportunity to change one thing about my job so I could be more effective, I know just what I'd pick.

People

- At work I am good at understanding people and making myself understood.

- I understand the strengths and weaknesses of the people around me and work accordingly.

- I feel good about how I work with the teams I work with.

- When I need someone to do something for me at work, I know how to ask in such a way that it generally gets done.

- When people get emotional at work, I can handle it in a way that's both kind and effective.

- I don't spend a lot of time in conflict with other people at work.

- People rarely "throw me off my game" at work.

- I've gotten my boss to a point where they basically understand what I do all day.

- No matter what size group of people I have to deal with—be it 1:1, a large group, or anywhere in between—I have strategies to deploy.

- I have been told I'm good at bringing new people into the organization or my specific team.

215

Technology

- I figure technology out by playing with it.

- I could explain in very basic terms what the main technology I touch at work is supposed to be used for.

- I have a basic understanding of how all of the technology I use at work works together.

- I'm curious about new technologies and go learn about them.

- I have a clear understanding of what the technologies I use can't do.

- If something goes wrong with a technology I use at work, I can sometimes fix it without calling IT.

- I could make some good, educated guesses about how technology might change my job in the next 5–10 years.

- I don't spend a lot of time at work fighting with technology, or getting freaked out by it.

- In general, if something can be done with the help of technology, I'll do it that way.

- When I explain to people how to do something at work, I can be very clear about how I utilize technology to do it.

Appendix: The Effectiveness Self-Assessment

Chapter 1: The Simple Power of Being Effective

1. NOAA. 2025. *Weather and Climate Influences on the January 2025 Fires Around Los Angeles*. NOAA Climate.gov. Accessed May 5, 2025.

2. Telling, Gillian. 2025. "Hero Meteorologist Saved Hundreds with His Early Fire Warnings. Here's What He's Worried About Next (Exclusive)." *People*, January 13, 2025.

3. Yu, Mallory, Ailsa Chang, and Christopher Intagliata. 2025. "Meet the 24-Year-Old 'Neighborhood Hero' Who Gave Early Warnings About the Eaton Fire." *NPR*, January 13, 2025.

4. @charllsmc. 2025. TikTok video, January 2025.

5. Gartland, Dan. 2020. "Utah Man Claims He Made and Delivered Michael Jordan's Fateful Pizza." *Sports Illustrated*, May 19, 2020.

6. Gallo, Carmine. 2013. "Public Speaking: How MLK Improvised the Second Half of the 'Dream' Speech." *Forbes*, August 27, 2013.

7. Panagiotakopoulos, Thanasi. 2024. "Your Lifetime Contract: How Career Earnings Can Add Up to Millions." *LifeManaged Financial Advisors*, December 3, 2024.

8. Maslach, Christina, and Susan E. Jackson. n.d. "Maslach Burnout Inventory – Human Services Survey (MBI-HSS)." *Mind Garden*. Accessed May 5, 2025.

9. Magono, Judith. 2025. "AI Is Getting Better, but Not Everywhere." *Medium*, January 2025.

10. U.S. Department of Labor. n.d. ONET OnLine*. Accessed May 5, 2025.

11. Lee, Bruce Y. 2020. "Electronic Health Records: Here Is How Much Time Doctors Are Spending with Them." *Forbes*, January 13, 2020.

12. Author unknown. n.d. "Why People Quit 90% of Online Classes—and How to Beat the Odds." *The Muse*. Accessed May 5, 2025.

13. Alfonseca, Kiara. 2019. "Crows Enjoy Using Tools, Researchers Find." *ABC News*, August 6, 2019.

Chapter 2: Building Your Effectiveness Architecture to Withstand a Changing World

1. Gratias, Melissa. 2025. "Bad at Doing What You Love." https://www .melissagratias.com/bad-at-doing-what-you-love/. Accessed August 4, 2025.

2. "The Convention." *The Office Wiki*. https://theoffice.fandom.com/wiki/ The_Convention. Accessed August 4, 2025.

3. "Survivor Man." *The Office Wiki*. https://theoffice.fandom.com/wiki/ Survivor_Man. Accessed August 4, 2025.

4. "Russell Bell." *The Wire Wiki*. https://thewire.fandom.com/wiki/Russell_ Bell. Accessed August 4, 2025.

5. O*NET OnLine. "Descriptor 1.C.3.c." https://www.onetonline.org/find/ descriptor/result/1.C.3.c. Accessed August 4, 2025.

Chapter 3: The Ground Floor of Your Effectiveness Architecture: Knowledge and Methods

1. *The Breakfast Club*. 1985. Directed by John Hughes. Universal Pictures. Clip from *Clip.cafe*. "Bender: Did You Know Without Trigonometry There'd Be No Engineering." https://clip.cafe/the-breakfast-club-1985/ bender-did-know-without-trigonometry-thered-be-no-engineering/. Accessed October 15, 2025.

2. *Idiocracy*. 2006. Directed by Mike Judge. 20th Century Fox. IMDb. https://www.imdb.com/title/tt0387808/. Accessed October 15, 2025.

3. The Taxi Academy. "History of the Knowledge." https://thetaxi.academy/history-of-the-knowledge/. Accessed August 4, 2025.

4. Matias I. Vidal and Hugo Spiers. "The Knowledge: A Test of London Taxi Drivers." *bioRxiv*, June 4, 2021. https://www.biorxiv.org/content/10.1101/2021.06.04.447168v1.full.pdf.

5. "The Knowledge." *CabbieBlog*. https://cabbieblog.com/the-knowledge/. Accessed August 4, 2025.

6. Michael Lewis. "Why Do Taxi Drivers in London Have to Memorize 25,000 Streets?" *New York Times*, November 10, 2014.

7. Alex Hern. "Ten Years of Google Maps: How It Changed the World." *The Guardian*, February 8, 2015.

8. "Black Taxi Fleet Size." https://www.london.gov.uk/who-we-are/what-london-assembly-does/questions-mayor/find-an-answer/black-taxi-fleet-size. Accessed August 4, 2025.

9. Damien Gayle. "London's Black Cabs 'Destined for Extinction in 20 Years,' TfL Warned." *The Guardian*, March 19, 2025. https://www.theguardian.com/uk-news/2025/mar/19/londons-black-cabs-destined-for-extinction-in-20-years-tfl-warned.

10. Robert Booth. "How Uber Conquered London." *The Guardian*, April 27, 2016.

11. "Uber Technologies Patents – Insights and Stats." *GreyB Insights*. https://insights.greyb.com/uber-technologies-patents/. Accessed August 4, 2025.

12. Ingrid Lunden. "Wayve and Uber Plan London Robotaxi Launch." *TechCrunch*, June 10, 2025.

13. Jake Klinger. "How Henry Ford Advocated for Roads—Until a Camping Club Beckoned." *Hagerty*, June 28, 2024. https://www.hagerty.com/media/automotive-history/how-henry-ford-advocated-for-public-road-building-until-he-wanted-to-join-a-fancy-camping-club/.

14. John W. Creswell. *Research Design: Qualitative, Quantitative, and Mixed Methods Approaches*, 4th ed. (Thousand Oaks, CA: SAGE, 2013). https://us.sagepub.com/sites/default/files/upm-binaries/42924_1.pdf.

Notes

15. "Richard Nixon and the Election of 1960." *Waverly High School Blog.* https://waverlyhs.weebly.com/us-history-blog-may-2016---may-2017/ richard-nixon-and-the-election-of-1960. Accessed August 4, 2025.

16. "Barbie (2023)—Full Transcript." *Scraps from the Loft.* 2023. https:// scrapsfromtheloft.com/movies/barbie-2023-transcript/.

Chapter 4: The Second Floor of Your Effectiveness Architecture: People and Technology

1. "Homo sapiens." *Smithsonian National Museum of Natural History: Human Origins.* https://humanorigins.si.edu/evidence/human-fossils/ species/homo-sapiens. Accessed August 4, 2025.

2. Jessica R. Li and Michael Varnum. "Revisiting the Collective Nature of Human Nature: The Evolutionary Psychology of Interdependence." *Current Research in Ecological and Social Psychology* 6 (2024). https:// www.sciencedirect.com/science/article/pii/S2950236524000173.

3. Marisa G. Franco. "The Whites of Your Eyes Are Proof You Need Connection." *Psychology Today*, January 2023. https://www .psychologytoday.com/us/blog/the-case-for-connection/202301/ the-whites-of-your-eyes-are-proof-you-need-connection.

4. Julian Jaynes. *The Origin of Consciousness in the Breakdown of the Bicameral Mind* (Boston, MA: Houghton Mifflin, 1976). https:// de2b5c91-0850-4c7e-8e5c-f454d5b74887.usrfiles.com/ugd/de2b5c_ 96d595dcfe444a26b635b48e74f01c42.pdf. Accessed August 4, 2025.

5. Robert I. Sutton. *The No Asshole Rule: Building a Civilized Workplace and Surviving One That Isn't* (New York: Business Plus, 2007). https:// www.gsb.stanford.edu/faculty-research/books/no-asshole-rule- building-civilized-workplace-surviving-one-isnt.

6. "Machiavellianism." *Psychology Today.* https://www.psychologytoday .com/us/basics/machiavellianism. Accessed August 4, 2025.

7. Roger Schwarz. "The Most Productive Meetings Have Fewer than 8 People." *Harvard Business Review*, June 2018. https://hbr.org/2018/06/the-most-productive-meetings-have-fewer-than-8-people.

8. Richard P. Feynman. *Surely You're Joking, Mr. Feynman!: Adventures of a Curious Character*, ed. Edward Hutchings (New York: W. W. Norton, 1985), 127.

9. "How Powerful Is a Dog's Nose?" *Phoenix Vet Center Blog.* https://phoenixvetcenter.com/blog/214731-how-powerful-is-a-dogs-nose. Accessed August 4, 2025.

Chapter 5: The Shockingly Consistent Playbook for Effectiveness in High-Stakes Jobs

1. *JO 7110.65 Air Traffic Control (FAA ATC/ATO Handbook)* (Washington, DC: U.S. Department of Transportation, Federal Aviation Administration, 2023). https://www.amazon.com/dp/9798388008770.

2. "ATC Simulator – Real Communications from Boston Center (ZBW)." YouTube video, 1:03:15, posted by VATUSA, November 4, 2021. https://www.youtube.com/watch?v=_2P6VuXHsqI.

3. Martha Mangelsdorf. "Zeynep Ton Makes the Case for Good Jobs." *MIT Sloan School of Management*, March 14, 2024. https://mitsloan.mit.edu/centers-initiatives/institute-work-and-employment-research/zeynep-ton-makes-case-good-jobs.

4. Institute of Medicine (US) Committee on Quality of Health Care in America. *Crossing the Quality Chasm: A New Health System for the 21st Century* (Washington, DC: National Academies Press, 2001). https://www.ncbi.nlm.nih.gov/books/NBK459369/.

5. Melissa Swift. "When Team Accountability Is Low: Four Hard Questions for Leaders." *MIT Sloan Management Review*, March 27, 2025. https://sloanreview.mit.edu/article/when-team-accountability-is-low-four-hard-questions-for-leaders/.

6. "The West Wing 6x01 – NSF Thurmont – Transcript." *Forever Dreaming Transcripts Forum.* https://transcripts.foreverdreaming.org/viewtopic.php?t=206843#google_vignette. Accessed August 4, 2025.

7. Roberto Torres. "Gartner: Digital Worker Tool Usage Up, but Tech Problems Persist." *CIO Dive*, March 7, 2023. https://www.ciodive.com/news/gartner-digital-worker-tools-IT/649844/.

Chapter 6: Effectiveness Through Battling Work Intensification

1. Andy Newman. "I Went Undercover Delivering for DoorDash, UberEats and More." *New York Times*, July 21, 2019. https://www.nytimes.com/2019/07/21/nyregion/doordash-ubereats-food-app-delivery-bike.html.

2. European Foundation for the Improvement of Living and Working Conditions, Sixth European Working Conditions Survey – Overview Report (Luxembourg: Publications Office of the European Union, 2016). https://www.eurofound.europa.eu/publications/report/2016/working-conditions/sixth-european-working-conditions-survey-overview-report.

3. Trades Union Congress (TUC). Work Intensification: An Initial Analysis of the Impact of Intensification on Workers and Unions, July 2023. https://www.tuc.org.uk/sites/default/files/2023-07/WorkIntensificationr ReportJuly2023.pdf.

4. Melissa Swift. Effectiveness in a Wild World of Work: Understanding and Combatting Work Intensification (New York: Anthrome Insight, 2025). https://de2b5c91-0850-4c7e-8e5c-f454d5b74887.usrfiles.com/ugd/de2b5c_96d595dcfe444a26b635b48e74f01c42.pdf.

5. Remesh Database. Exploring Our Experiences at Work. Complete May 1, 2025.

6. Swift, *Effectiveness in a Wild World of Work*, 2025.

7. Chip Cutter. "The Vanishing Executive Assistant." *Wall Street Journal*, October 22, 2023.

8. Swift, *Effectiveness in a Wild World of Work*, 2025.

9. Carleton English. "Jamie Dimon Urges JPMorgan Employees to Return to the Office." *Barron's*, April 14, 2023. https://www.barrons.com/articles/jamie-dimon-leaked-audio-jpmorgan-return-to-office-7064ee64.

10. Dana R. Vashdi, Jingqiu Chen, Qingyue Fan, and Peter A. Bamberger. "Supportive but Exhausting: A Dual-Path Model of Team Interdependence and Member Negative Emotional States." *Journal of Business and Psychology*, 39(5), 2024: 1–19. https://doi.org/10.1007/s10869-024-09937-8. https://www.researchgate.net/publication/378365143.

11. Swift, *Effectiveness in a Wild World of Work*, 2025.

12. Scott A. Golder. "Hours and the Workweek." MIT CSAIL. https://groups.csail.mit.edu/mac/users/rauch/worktime/hours_workweek.html. Accessed August 4, 2025.

13. Tim Fernholz. "The Rise and Fall of American Productivity Growth." *Quartz*, April 14, 2016. https://qz.com/633080/the-rise-and-fall-of-american-productivity-growth.

14. Melissa Swift. "How Leaders Fight Back Against Overwork." *MIT Sloan Management Review*, June 30, 2025. https://sloanreview.mit.edu/article/how-leaders-fight-back-against-overwork/.

15. Swift, *Effectiveness in a Wild World of Work*, 2025.

16. Swift, *How Leaders Fight Back Against Overwork*, 2025.

17. Nikolaus Obwegeser and Markus H. Blut. "Organizational Complexity as a Contributing Factor to Underperformance." *ResearchGate*, December 2022. https://www.researchgate.net/publication/365775017_Organizational_Complexity_as_a_Contributing_Factor_to_Underperformance.

18. Swift, "When Team Accountability Is Low: Four Hard Questions for Leaders." *MIT Sloan Management Review*, March 27, 2025. https://sloanreview.mit.edu/article/when-team-accountability-is-low-four-hard-questions-for-leaders/.

19. Swift, *Effectiveness in a Wild World of Work*, 2025.

20. Jennifer Elias. "Google CEO Tells Employees Productivity and Focus Must Improve." *CNBC*, July 31, 2022. https://www.cnbc.com/2022/07/31/google-ceo-to-employees-productivity-and-focus-must-improve.html.

Notes

21. Robert I. Sutton and Huggy Rao. *The Friction Project: How Smart Leaders Make the Right Things Easier and the Wrong Things Harder* (New York: St. Martin's Press, 2024). https://bobsutton.net/book/the-friction-project/.

Chapter 7: Effectiveness Through Managing Workplace Emotion Appropriately

1. NASA. *Behavioral Health Mishaps: Technical Brief OCHMO-TB-014 Rev. B* (Washington, DC: NASA Office of the Chief Health & Medical Officer, October 31, 2023). https://www.nasa.gov/wp-content/uploads/2023/12/ochmo-tb-014-behavioral-health-mishaps.pdf.

2. R. Alan Leo. "Atmospheric Disturbance." *Harvard Medicine Magazine*, July 2024. https://magazine.hms.harvard.edu/articles/atmospheric-disturbance

3. "Worker Negative Emotions Stay Above Pre-Pandemic Levels." *Gallup*. https://www.gallup.com/workplace/653708/worker-negative-emotions-stay-above-pre-pandemic-levels.aspx. Accessed August 5, 2025.

4. Remesh Database. *Exploring Our Experiences at Work*. Complete May 1, 2025.

5. "Conflict Trends: Global Overview 1946–2023." *ReliefWeb*. https://reliefweb.int/report/world/conflict-trends-global-overview-1946-2023. Accessed August 5, 2025.

6. "Political Parties Historically Polarized Ideologically." *Gallup*. https://news.gallup.com/poll/655190/political-parties-historically-polarized-ideologically.aspx. Accessed August 5, 2025.

7. "Modern Workplace Communication." *Preply*. https://preply.com/en/blog/modern-workplace-communication/. Accessed August 5, 2025.

8. "Technostress: How Too Much Technology Affects Mental Health." *Kaiser Permanente My Doctor News*. https://mydoctor.kaiserpermanente.org/mas/news/technostress-how-too-much-technology-effects-mental-health-2054999. Accessed August 5, 2025.

9. "Psychosocial Safety Climate as a Lead Indicator of Workplace Health and Performance: A Review and Conceptual Model." *PMC (NCBI)*. 2014. https://pmc.ncbi.nlm.nih.gov/articles/PMC4134534/.

10. CartoonStock. "Search Results for 'CS211910' Cartoon." https://www
.cartoon?stock.com/cartoon?searchID=CS211910. Accessed August 5, 2025.

11. YouTube video. "_RujOFCHsxo." https://www.youtube.com/watch?v=_
RujOFCHsxo. Accessed August 5, 2025.

12. YouTube video. "6M8szlSa-8o." https://www.youtube.com/watch?v=
6M8szlSa-8o. Accessed August 5, 2025.

Chapter 8: Effectiveness Through Harnessing Transparency Properly

1. Paycor. "Pay Transparency Laws by State." *Paycor*, n.d. https://www
.paycor.com/resource-center/articles/pay-transparency-laws-by-state/.

2. Glassdoor. "About Us." *Glassdoor*, n.d. https://www.glassdoor.com/about/

3. Glassdoor. "Vulcan Materials Reviews." *Glassdoor*, n.d. https://www
.glassdoor.com/Reviews/Vulcan-Materials-Reviews-E709.htm.

4. DemandSage. "Slack Statistics (2025): Users, Revenue, Market Share,
Facts." *DemandSage*, September 2025. https://www.demandsage.com/
slack-statistics/.

5. Swift, Melissa. "Leading in the Age of Exploding Transparency." MIT
Sloan Management Review, November 29, 2023. https://sloanreview.mit.edu/
article/leading-in-the-age-of-exploding-transparency/.

6. Reddit user u/jackisoon. "TIL Mushroom Management Is Where
Employees Aren't Given Enough Information to Do Their Job, Then Are
Kept in the Dark and Fed Bullshit." *Reddit*, March 24, 2020. https://
www.reddit.com/r/todayilearned/comments/fsz63x/til_mushroom_
management_is_where_employees_arent/.

7. Fishbowl. "Invent NA – so who's going to run the numbers of % of
presenters and year end award nominees on the All Hands that were POC."
Comment from Capgemini. Accessed September 30, 2025.

8. Xiang, Beike, Qinghua Ma, Hongxia Ma, Xiaonan Zhang, and Pengcheng
Sun. "Exploring the Mediating Role of Psychological Capital in the
Relationship between Organizational Justice and Work Engagement."
BMC Psychology, 12(1), (2024). https://bmcpsychology.biomedcentral.com/
articles/10.1186/s40359-024-01966-5.

9. Raconteur. "Big Debate: Is Office Gossip Good or Bad for Business?" *Raconteur*, October 26, 2021. https://www.raconteur.net/talent-culture/big-debate-office-gossip.

10. Swift, Melissa. "Four Leadership Loads That Keep Getting Heavier." MIT Sloan Management Review, December 2, 2024. https://sloanreview.mit.edu/article/four-leadership-loads-that-keep-getting-heavier/.

11. Pew Research Center. "Social Media and the Workplace." Pew Research Center: Internet, Science & Tech, June 22, 2016. https://www.pewresearch.org/internet/2016/06/22/social-media-and-the-workplace/.

12. McCullough, David. The Johnstown Flood (New York: Simon & Schuster, 1968), 100.

13. Johnstown Area Heritage Association. "Facts about the 1889 Flood." Johnstown Flood Museum, n.d. https://www.heritagejohnstown.org/attractions/johnstown-flood-museum/flood-history/facts-about-the-1889-flood/.

Chapter 9: Effectiveness Through Wrestling Down Chaos

1. Fractal Foundation. "What Is Chaos Theory?" Fractal Foundation, n.d. https://fractalfoundation.org/resources/what-is-chaos-theory/.

2. Caroline Tremblay. "Garrett Morgan: The Man Who Changed Traffic." *AAA Northeast Magazine*, February 2023. https://magazine.northeast.aaa.com/daily/life/cars-trucks/auto-history/garrett-morgan-traffic-signal/.

3. Lyt. "Who Invented Traffic Lights?" *Lyt Blog*, June 27, 2023. https://lyt.ai/blog/on-the-road/who-invented-traffic-lights/.

4. National Safety Council. "Motor Vehicle Deaths, 1899–2022." *Injury Facts*, n.d. https://injuryfacts.nsc.org/motor-vehicle/historical-fatality-trends/deaths-and-rates/.

5. Tremblay (2023).

6. Adams, Bill. "Chaos in the House: Managing Workplace Complexity." *Forbes*, July 25, 2022. https://www.forbes.com/sites/forbesbooksauthors/2022/07/25/chaos-in-the-house-managing-workplace-complexity/.

7. U.S. Bureau of Labor Statistics. "Business Employment Dynamics: Establishment Size Data." Bureau of Labor Statistics, n.d. https://www.bls.gov/bdm/bdmfirmsize.htm.

8. Walmart. 1995 Annual Report (New York: Walmart Inc., 1995). https://www.annualreports.com/HostedData/AnnualReportArchive/w/NYSE_WMT_1995_5d4a09556490442f968e9a557119b28b.pdf.

9. The Home Depot. 1995 Annual Report. (Atlanta, GA: The Home Depot, 1995). https://ir.homedepot.com/~/media/Files/H/HomeDepot-IR/Annual%20Reports/1995%20Annual%20Report.pdf.

10. HistoryLink. "Garrett Morgan, African American Inventor of the Traffic Signal, Patents His Device on November 20, 1923." HistoryLink.org, September 8, 2022. https://www.historylink.org/File/23230.

11. U.S. Census Bureau. "Population Change Data (Text Files)." United States Census Bureau, n.d. https://www.census.gov/data/tables/time-series/dec/popchange-data-text.html.

12. Karolina Mania. "Organizational Complexity as a Contributing Factor to Underperformance." ResearchGate, November 2022. https://www.researchgate.net/publication/365775017_Organizational_Complexity_as_a_Contributing_Factor_to_Underperformance.

13. Andis Robeznieks. "Biggest Match Day Ever? Here's What 2025 Numbers Reveal." American Medical Association, March 14, 2025. https://www.ama-assn.org/medical-students/preparing-residency/biggest-match-day-ever-here-s-what-2025-numbers-reveal.

14. José María Soriano, Antoni Moliner-Urdiales, and Mariona Comas. "Effect of COVID-19 Lockdown on Physical Activity and Sedentary Behaviour in Spanish University Students: A Longitudinal Study." *International Journal of Environmental Research and Public Health*, 18(6), (2021). https://pmc.ncbi.nlm.nih.gov/articles/PMC8300849/.

15. Roscigno, Vincent J., Randy Hodson, and Steven H. Lopez. "Workplace Incivilities: The Role of Interest Conflicts, Social Closure, and Organizational Chaos." *Work, Employment & Society*, 23(4), (2009): 747–773. https://doi.org/10.1177/0950017009344875.

16. Roscigno et al. (2009).

Notes

17. MIT Sloan School of Management. "Zeynep Ton Makes the Case for Good Jobs." MIT Sloan School of Management: Institute for Work and Employment Research, March 27, 2024. https://mitsloan.mit.edu/centers-initiatives/institute-work-and-employment-research/zeynep-ton-makes-case-good-jobs.

18. Roscigno et al. (2009).

19. Lithwick, Dahlia. "What Is Chaos Theory? A Unified Theory of Muppet Types." *Slate*, June 8, 2012. https://slate.com/life/2012/06/chaos-theory.html.

20. University of California, Berkeley. "Impact of Interruptions." UC Berkeley People & Culture, n.d. https://hr.berkeley.edu/grow/grow-your-community/wisdom-caf%C3%A9-wednesday/impact-interruptions.

21. Lithwick (2012).

22. A. O. Scott. "What Chaos Really Means." *New York Times*, September 12, 2024. https://www.nytimes.com/interactive/2024/09/12/books/chaos-meaning-word.html.

Chapter 10: What to Do (Next) When Effectiveness Is Not Possible

1. KCYesterday. "The Story of Harry Truman's (Failed) Haberdashery in KC." *KCYesterday*, December 5, 2024. https://kcyesterday.com/articles/harry-trumans-failed-haberdashery?srsltid=AfmBOopSWCsPJTV25-ub6fdwVAi0mUB8YKK-FJ4IaBXMfsREscU2OJBvB.

2. JNS. "Edward Jacobson (1891–1965)." *JNS*, March 14, 2018. https://www.jns.org/edward-jacobson-1891-1965/.

3. Watkins, Dylan. "Teachers Spend a Staggering Amount on School Supplies." *USA Today*, August 30, 2025. https://www.usatoday.com/story/money/2025/08/30/how-much-teacher-spending-school-supplies/85830237007/.

4. Bender, Kristin. "Bad Bosses Push Gen Zers and Millennials to the Brink of Quitting." *Fortune*, August 9, 2024. https://fortune.com/2024/08/09/bad-bosses-push-gen-z-millennials-to-brink-of-quitting/.

In the context of this book, as in life in general, I have a lot of folks to thank.

A massive thank you to the more than 20 brilliant folks from the corporate, public service, consulting, and academic worlds who generously gave their time to be interviewed for this book. Individually and collectively, you all not only contributed fabulous quotes, but more fundamentally helped shape my thinking on an array of important topics. Rarely has my brain grown so much as during these interviews—and I think you'll have the same impact on the readers of this book. Anthony Tisdall, Birke Bakker, Courtney Chisholm, Dimitris Bountolos, Dustin Liu, Isabella Loiaza, Jim Detert, Joao Goncalves, Laura Fisher, Maria Amato, Mark Polansky, Mary Cianni, Michelle Stuntz, Ramy Houssaini, Dr. Rebecca Parker, Rick McDonald, Roland Rodriguez, Suzy Welch, Tauseef Rahman, Teryluz Andreu, Thiago Licias de Oliveira, Tom Peck, and Vipin Gupta—thank you for your thinking and your inspiration. And a special meta thank you to Michelle Stuntz, Laurie McLaughlin, and Jaclyn Roster, respectively, who answered my call for "an air traffic controller, an ER doctor, and a firefighter" with outstanding folks from their networks, and made Chapter 4 possible.

I'm also lucky to have worked with a wonderful team at Wiley—for the second time! Zach Schisgal, Amanda Pyne, Michelle Hacker,

Kim Wimpsett, and Deborah Schindler all care deeply about books and really helped put the work and inspiration in to get to a compelling finished product. It takes a village, and the Wiley village rocks.

Getting a book seen in a noisy, crowded world is no small feat. Working with the disciplined, inspired (but also fun and really nice!) folks at Book Highlight has given me such confidence in this book's ability to break through the clutter. Peter Knox, Brian Morrison, Alana Whitman, Deidra Higgins, and Christian Tysklind—your effectiveness and kindness have made my day so many days.

Tess Woods of Tess Woods PR, and her terrific co-worker Cjay Yu, define "indefatigable" in my book (literally and figuratively, I guess!). You are pitbulls on the pantleg of the media and podcast world, and I am so delighted to benefit from your creativity and tenacity.

MIT Sloan Management Review has transformed my writing life. It has long been my dream to write for a top-tier business publication but honestly, I never thought I would even get close. Thanks to the extraordinary sponsorship of Abbie Lundberg and Laurie McLaughlin, I first became a columnist and more recently, a member of their Editorial Review Board. This is one of the great honors of my life and, as a bonus, working with Laurie as an editor has made me a far better writer.

The MIT CIO Symposium, where I've had the honor of being a speaker several times, is also a key player in the "origin story" of this book. Allan Tate, Irving Wladawsky-Berger, Tina Kruczynski, Chasity Meade, George Westerman, and Lindsay Anderson—thank you for including me and you will see the fingerprints of the CIO Symposium on the interview list above. What you won't see is that at a symposium many years ago I met Ginny Holden, who encouraged me to write for a publication regularly for the first time (thank you Ginny!) and then introduced me to Laurie McLaughlin; at the same symposium I was introduced to Abbie Lundberg by the wonderful Mark

Polansky (who gets props as a people connector in this book). The CIO Symposium truly brings great folks together.

Having left the corporate world for entrepreneurship, friends were more important this year than ever before. And I have the most terrific ones—alphabetically: Alexa, Andrea, Carol, Jaclyn, Julie, Maria, Mary, Michelle, Parul, Shari, Stacie, and Vijaya. I appreciate you all so much for just being willing to talk, supporting me in tough moments, and periodically making me cackle with laughter. It can be a fragmented world out there, but I feel surrounded by connection, thanks to you guys.

A huge thank you to my clients, past and present. If I've learned anything about organizations, it has been from you. Thank you for trusting me with important, complicated, difficult work, and for so often making me feel like a part of your team.

And a similar thank you to so many of my former co-workers. So much of my personal effectiveness has been because really talented people agreed to work with me. As I told one of you the other day, working with outstanding people feels like a videogame "cheat code"—making work so much easier and more fun.

Special shout outs:

- Hope King, who has—in between the last book and this one— switched categories from "incredible journalist who unknow- ingly helped get me onto the book publishing radar" to "awesome friend who's on her own entrepreneurial journey." Rooting for you, dude.

- Laura Kelfer, who is not quoted in this book as such but from whom I have learned a ton by working together—thus her bril- liance is infused throughout!

- Taylor Frey, who basically framed up for me exactly what this book needs to be for its readers. Your insight and support mean so much.

Acknowledgments

- Patrick Hyland, who is not just an awesome former co-worker, but also my co-brain on the work-intensification study that features prominently in Chapter 5 (and thanks Remesh for the amazing study platform).

- Three former bosses, who pushed me to be more than I aspired to be at the time I worked for them: Dave Pearson, Mary Cianni, and Sandeep Bhatia. It continues to warm my heart every day that each of you saw something in me and stated that clearly and assertively. I hope to live up to your views.

Finally, my family. Thanks Mom for being a role model of a powerful woman at work. Thanks to my wonderful husband Artem, who is both my mental model of an effective corporate executive but also as kind and intelligent a person as you could ever hope to have in your life. And thank you to my daughter Mira—someday you'll hit the working world like a tornado, but right now you are just the best middle schooler on the planet.

About the Author

Melissa Swift is a leading voice on how organizations, teams, and individuals can succeed in an ever more challenging world of work. As founder and CEO of Anthrome Insight, she is a practicing consultant and keynote speaker helping organizations with data-driven views and concrete strategies to shape a productive future in chaotic times. She has held consulting leadership roles at Capgemini, Mercer, Korn Ferry, and Deloitte, and is the author of *Work Here Now: Think Like a Human and Build a Powerhouse Workplace*, as well as the current title.

Throughout her career, Melissa has leveraged unconventional analytics and broken down traditional people consulting siloes to provide actionable guidance on topics such as the organizational side of digital transformation and the changing nature of leadership in the C-suite and beyond. Both a humanist and a pragmatist, Melissa has continually explored the balance of maximizing human potential and worker health while simultaneously achieving outstanding business outcomes.

Melissa is a member of the *MIT Sloan Management Review*'s Editorial Board and one of the publication's most widely read columnists. She has been featured in *The New York Times*, *The Wall Street Journal*, the *Financial Times*, *Newsweek*, and a host of other prestigious publications, as well as appearances on NPR (National Public Radio). Melissa was named in the Thinkers50 Radar class of

2023, and *Work Here Now* appeared on awards lists from McKinsey and Porchlight Books. She holds a BA from Harvard University and an MBA from Columbia Business School.

Melissa lives in New York City with her husband, daughter, and neurotic beagle.

Index

EFFECTIVE EXCELLENCE

Do great work with the latest resources and support from Melissa Swift:

- Articles
- Research
- Media
- Video
- Effectiveness Assessment
- Beyond the Book Activities

anthromeinsight.com